Reclaiming The American Democratic Impulse

Laurie Thomas Vass

The Great American Business &
Economics Press© GabbyPress©

Revised 2023.

Publisher: The Great American Business
& Economics Press. (GABBY Press) ©

ISBN
979-8-218-13511-9

Table of Contents

Introduction: After Obama.

In his recent book, The Liberty Amendments, Mark Levin promotes the enactment of 10 amendments to the U. S. Constitution, using the second method of amendment outlined in Article V, of the Constitution of 1788. (The Liberty Amendments: Restoring the American Republic, 2014.).

While his suggested amendments could possibly offer relief from the dysfunction in the American political system, his suggestions contain two debilitating flaws that would not remedy the loss of individual freedoms from the tyranny of Obama's centralized, socialist government power.

First, Levin's ideas are not viable for enactment, using the second method of amendment.

As he notes,

"the second method has never been successfully implemented in over 230 years."

Levin offers no clues to how or why he thinks this second path of amendment would be successful with his proposed amendments.

The second method of amendment was deliberately made unviable by Madison and the Federalists because they feared the political instability of non-elite citizens intervening in the constitutional process.

Second, even granting Levin the benefit of the doubt that all of his amendments were successfully enacted, Levin's remedy contains the mistaken assumption that the socialists, or statists, as he calls them, would immediately change their behavior and begin to abide by the rule of law.

Levin goes through the entire historical chronology of how Obama undermined the rule of law in the current constitution, but assumes that with the enactment of his amendments, that socialists, like Obama or Hillary, would begin to follow the new rules.

Socialists will never follow constitutional rules because socialism is a religious belief, and socialists do not follow rules made by non-socialists.

The socialists are driven by the moral imperatives of their religion, and seek to impose their religious views on non-socialists.

Non-socialists, from the viewpoint of the socialist religion, are heretics and bad people, not morally worthy to make rules or govern themselves.

In the socialist religion, only the non-socialists are bound by the laws that are made by the socialists. Socialists call this idea "smart growth," or some other label that conveys that socialists are smarter than the common herd.

A more realistic appraisal of socialists is that they are not bound by constitutional law because the constitution contains principles of individual freedom, which are inconsistent with their collectivist religion of elite rule.

Levin's amendments also assume that, after the enactment of his amendments, that the Republican Party would adopt new policy positions to defend liberty.

Levin mistakenly assumes that there would be something of social cultural value to restore in the wreckage of individual liberty inflicted by Obama, and that the

Republicans would defend the remaining cultural values.

The Republican Party long ago abandoned defending the concept of individual liberty, long ago abdicated their historical responsibility to defend American culture from the socialist onslaught.

Just like the Democrat response of not changing behavior after Levin's proposed amendments, the Republicans are not going to suddenly change into a middle class political movement that defends liberty.

We argue that a better idea for restoring individual liberty is to start over at the point in history of Jefferson's Declaration, with a new constitution that makes preserving individual liberty the mission of the new government.

The solution to the restoration of liberty in America is more citizen democracy, not less democracy.

Citizens lack the power to alter or amend Madison's flawed set of rules.

In other words, citizens today are helpless politically to reclaim their Spirit of Liberty from the existing two-party framework.

The most severe flaw of the Federalist Constitution was their deliberate omission in the Preamble that the ultimate goal of the constitution was to protect individual freedoms.

This flaw of omitting the end goal results in a dysfunctional government is commonly described as the "Arrow Paradox." (Arrow, Kenneth Joseph, Social Choice and Individual Values, 1951.).

The Paradox means that, in the absence of a constitutional end goal, the political system cycles over and over again, in a do-loop, that results in mistakes continually being repeated because there is no bright line definition of the constitutional public purpose.

A more 'perfect union" could mean the loss of individual freedom, and the imposition of socialists tyranny, if the socialists ever managed to win control of the government.

Or, the phrase "insure domestic tranquility" could easily mean using the police power of the deep state to target and punish political enemies, such as the farmers in Shays' Rebellion, in 1788, or MAGA supporters in 2022.

The socialists can fundamentally transform America into a socialist state because the Federalists did not proclaim that individual liberty was the end goal of their work.

Levin's amendments do not add the required philosophical Preamble end goal that would remedy the Federalist's flaws.

This book examines how a new constitution, which includes both Levin's suggested amendments, and the telos of liberty as the end goal, would be a better path than his idea of amending Madison's hopelessly broken representative republic.

That pathway to freedom means reclaiming the American Democratic Impulse.

Chapter 1: The American Democratic Impulse.

The accepted political wisdom in American political history is that the founding fathers set up a representative republic to avoid the excesses of a populist citizen's democracy.

The basic premise of the accepted wisdom is that individual citizens, in their capacity as voters, are too volatile and unreliable in judgments about civic affairs, and that any type of citizen's democracy would likely end up in "mob-rule."

There is another American political tradition that embraces the ability of individual citizens to make good decisions in a constitutional democratic republic.

Sean Wilentz, in his monumental work, The Rise of American Democracy: Jefferson to Lincoln, has called this other tradition the "American democratic impulse."

Wilenz asks,

"...how had the Jacksonian ascendancy shaped, for better and for worse, the democratic impulses that had arisen out of the American Revolution and had evolved so furiously after 1815?"(Wilentz, Sean, The Rise of American Democracy: Jefferson to Lincoln, W. W. Norton & Co., Inc., 2005.).

This other tradition has a legitimate claim as the correct interpretation of the American history of exceptionalism, meaning that the American experiment in promoting individual liberty is an exceptional event in human history.

The American democratic impulse derives its status of historical legitimacy from the words of Thomas Jefferson, in the Declaration of Independence.

The democratic tradition has been at the heart of the political heritage of three historical populist democratic political movements: the anti-federalists, of 1787, the Jacksonians of 1832, and the southern agrarian populists of 1885.

It is a political philosophy based upon the notion of individualism and equality of political rights.

The two great political philosophies in conflict in America are not defined by liberalism or conservatism.

The conflict in America is defined by those who believe in individualism and those who believe in collectivism.

In the hands of either the Democrats or Republicans, the increasing power of government leads to a loss of individual liberty.

This book takes a closer look at the goals advocated by the anti-federalists, the Jacksonians, and the agrarian farmers.

The book makes the claim that more individualism and more citizen democracy, within the state sovereignty tradition, is a valid historical tradition to rely upon in creating a new constitution.

The book also examines the conflict between Andrew Jackson and The Second Bank to see what constitutional lessons can be learned about special interest political market behavior of special interests, especially those financial interests of the national bank involved in manipulation of the money supply and interest rates.

Jackson's followers thought that by adopting stronger government regulations of the Second National Bank, a private bank which controlled the supply of money, that common citizens would have a better opportunity to control their own economic destiny.

Jackson's followers used the political phrase *"Equal Rights for All. Special Privileges for None,"* to promote their cause.

One of the purposes of government, according to this line of thought, was to protect the economically weak from the financially strong.

The power of government, the Jacksonians thought, could be used to provide a countervailing power to the economic power wielded by financial special interests who had organized into a political coalition, at first called Federalists, later called Whigs, and currently called Republicans.

Those political interests who opposed Jackson also had their own philosophy of government, which highlighted the benefits of the free market as complementary component to the American political system.

In their view, a strong national bank would contribute to individual freedom because the bank would facilitate economic growth and world trade.

One of the purposes of government, seen from the Federalist vantage point, is to create, and then legally protect, private

economic institutions in their function of promoting economic growth.

It was from these two political traditions, one favoring limits on private economic power, and one favoring free enterprise, that the current special interest two party system, in practice today, originated.

At ceremonial occasions for both parties, like national conventions, echoes of these earlier traditions are invoked by both Democrats and Republicans.

Both political factions wanted to use the power of government to accomplish different ends of society.

In both cases, as described by Larry Schweikart, in Banking in the American South from the Age of Jackson to Reconstruction, (LSU Press, 1987.), the use of government as an instrument to achieve social ends led to increased centralized political control over the workings of both the free market and the institutions of government.

Government power, in the hands of Jackson's Democratic Party, was effective in killing the Bank.

In the hands of the Whig Party, political power led to increased and concentrated private economic power, primarily used by financial institutions to enforce legal contracts involving mortgages and liens on farm property.

Either political party, then and now, could have claimed historical legitimacy about the purpose of government, as defined in the Preamble of Madison's Constitution, because the constitution failed to state the public purpose of government.

A more perfect union could be either outcome, depending on which political party controlled the U. S. Supreme Court.

While the relationship between politics and private economics served as a focal point for much of the discussion of those engaged in the making of the Constitution, the founders, and in particular, James

Madison, concentrated more on developing rules of civil procedure on how the braches of government should function, rather than on defining the constitutional public purpose served by government.

Madison's rules of procedure are very much like the rules of civil procedure in the American court system.

Madison's rules of procedure were aimed at achieving social class political equilibrium between competing economic and financial interests, where an independent federal judiciary made rulings on social class conflict.

The rules would work well, according to Madison, if they were both created and enforced by representatives from the natural aristocracy.

Madison's rules of governmental procedure tended to concentrate political power at the level of the Federal government, to the detriment of the states.

His rules contained a system of institutional checks and balances designed to limit despotic behavior by elected representatives at the Federal level.

The supremacy at the Federal level of rules, in Madison's philosophy, would overcome the corruption that he perceived in the operation of state governments.

However, according to Madison's constitutional design, the elected federal representatives had to be drawn from the ranks of the aristocracy.

Madison's constitution was about governance of special interests, not about democratic citizen participation in government.

In the late 1880's, an organization of American citizens, primarily farmers from the South and Southwest, recognized that the existing system of agricultural debt peonage was unfair.

Like Andrew Jackson's followers, the farmers initially focused on a series of political reforms, called the Ocala Platform, which were intended to correct the abuses they saw in both the political and economic systems.

The intent of the reforms primarily were directed at curbing the concentration of political power exercised by financial and industrial corporations by providing for stronger government regulations of market behavior.

One of the leaders of the southern agrarian revolt, Tom Watson, of Georgia, revived the phrase *"Equal Rights for All. Special Privileges for None,"* and placed it in the masthead of his newspaper.

In this later historical setting, the main target of reform was the repeal of legislation which deployed the resources of government to enforce the debt-peonage contracts that were limiting the ability of common citizens to ever get out of debt.

About 40 years earlier, a group of political reformers, upset about the Whigs support of slavery, and the Democrat's advocacy of the slaveocracy power in the U. S. Senate, coined a variation of the phrase.

Their use of the phrase was contained in a political document entitled "An Appeal of the Independent Democrats In Congress to the People of the United States," written in 1854.

In their appeal, they wrote,

"We entreat you to be mindful of that fundamental maxim of Democracy – Equal Rights and Exact Justice For All Men."

As Wilenz points out, the defenders of the slaveocracy contended that the antislavery movement demonstrated convincingly why common citizens should never be allowed to participate in governmental decisions.

Reviving the use of this political phrase, *Equal Rights For All. Special Priveleges for None,"* as a guide for constitutional reform, is part of the story of this book.

The common thread throughout the history of the American democratic impulse is the objective of implementing a political system that features equal political individual rights and special financial privileges for none.

The dynamic of American history captured by the motto is the continuing conflict between individuals who want to extend democracy and the politically organized special financial interests in both parties who oppose the extension of citizen populist democracy.

One of the major flaws in Madison's rules of procedure was accurately described by the conventions delegate, James Wilson.

Wilson asked many times, according to Robert Dahl, in How Democratic Is The American Constitution, "should the democratic government be designed to serve the "imaginary beings" called states, or should it be designed to serve the interests of all citizens?" (Yale University Press, 2003.).

Madison and Hamilton chose the synthetic and collectivistic interests of the government, as if the agencies of government were actually "We, the people."

Another part of the story told in this book, is that the current two party system will never yield the desired intent of the political reforms of citizen political equality because the political reforms advocated in this book imply greater citizen democracy, and concomitantly, less special interest control over government.

Both political parties are deeply invested in maintaining the status quo arrangement of special interest manipulation.

Yet, the mechanics of the system of government, written by Madison and Hamilton, makes the reform of the two party system impossible.

As it developed in time, the "first-past-the-post" voting system leads to a stable two party system, where third parties can never gain a competitive foothold.

The way the votes are counted, plus the insulation of the citizen's will in the Electoral College, means that the existing two party special interest system has a permanent lock on the American political landscape.

By the early 1890's, the leaders of the agrarian revolt had come to the conclusion that Madison's constitutional framework of making and enforcing the laws were loaded against the extension of democratic equality of common citizens.

Madison's carefully devised concept of a representative republic had succeeded too well in insulating the influence of the common citizens on the workings of the political system.

Once in place, Madison's system of insulation provided no remedy for the citizens to reassert control over the special interest manipulation that Madison's rules of procedure had created.

As Gordon Wood has pointed out in The Creation of the American Republic, not only did Madison's scheme provide for a system dominated by,

"...natural leaders who knew better than the people as a whole what was good for society, but it also succeeded in removing the non-natural leaders from the political process." (University of North Carolina Press, 1969.).

Wood noted,

"In fact, the people did not actually participate in government any more...The American (Federalists) had taken the people out of the government altogether. The true distinction of the American government wrote Madison in the Federalist 'lies in the total exclusion of the people, in their collective capacity, from any share in the government.'"

By the turn of the 20th century, Madison's scheme had allowed special interest elites to capture and control both the internal workings of each political party, and to infuse both the agencies of government, and the U. S. Supreme Court, with their partisans.

This dual position of power, over the political party system and the agencies of government, allowed the special interests to effectively shut off or control the direction of political reform to suit their elite interests.

The elite financial interests were interchangeable with the national public purpose because Madison's rules did not define liberty as the public purpose.

Madison's rules lead to the Arrow Paradox of recycling defects over and over again, with no viable solution.

The grid lock leads to a lack of consensus on what promotes the common wealth of the nation, and as will be seen later, it is this lack of national consensus on the issue of citizen sovereignty that constitutes the most urgent and immediate threat to citizen's fundamental rights.

The framers of the Constitution had discussed the topic of elite political control of the government at length.

John Adams wrote about the issue in his book, Thoughts on Government, and devoted considerable attention to the problem of how wealthy people could be enticed to continue to make investments that would lead to social prosperity, while at the same time avoiding a

"...system that rewarded, not skill and hard work, but family connections and political scheming."(Liberal Arts Press, 1954.).

Alexander Hamilton's obsession with gaining the nationalistic loyalty of the wealthy classes led him, in Federalist #15, to conclude that,

"...only coercion of individuals was effective in upholding national interests."

Of course, from Hamilton's point of view, the definition of "national interests" was solely left in the hands of the natural aristocracy.

In his review of Hamilton's work, Richard Bernstein posed the basic political question addressed by Madison and Hamilton:

"Was it dangerous in a democratic government, to have important officers insulated from control by the people, or was it necessary to accept that risk in order to protect fundamental rights from infringement by popular passions or political intrigue?" (Bernstein, Richard B., The Founding Fathers: A Very Short Introduction, Oxford University Press, 2015.).

The fundamental rights Bernstein refers to are the rights of the ruling class, not the rights of "all the people."

The elimination of citizen democratic control in national politics has led to special interest corruption controlled by the two major political parties.

For the Democrats, partisan politics means the continual invocation of class war and racial injustice as a political ploy to gain elected positions.

Their favorite political formula from their political strategy play book is that the rich are getting richer, poor people and minorities are victims who have grievances, and if Democrats are elected, these downtrodden helpless citizens may be able to get reparations and redress for their woes from their champions in the government.

For the Democrats, individual citizens must be lumped together into a collectivist social class system in order to be protected.

Individuals are perceived as helpless, but if they can just group themselves into classes, defined by their grievances, then their patrons, the Democrats, can direct government benefits their way.

Once they win elections, the elected Democrats return to their task of extracting financial gain for themselves from other citizens.

They have no conception of the "public purpose" or how to achieve the "common good."

The end goal of the socialist religion is the attainment of power to direct financial benefits to the socialist elites.

For the Republicans, partisan politics means implementing a type of Corporate Crony Big Government, with high taxes for the middle classes, that benefits large corporations and the wealthy ruling classes of America.

In the hands of Republicans, the Government would hand out welfare to the favored corporations, shift the tax burden to middle class citizens, and skew national foreign policy to the interests of the multinational corporations who promote the military industrial complex.

The Republicans actually have a conception of the public good that informs their political operations, in contrast to the Democrats' philosophical vacuity.

The Republicans do not often state it in public, and if they do state it, it is with much circumlocution.

The purpose of government for Republicans echoes the earlier Whig philosophy, that the public good is obtained when private corporations have the greatest freedom to use the agencies of government for private corporate purposes.

They usually use the term "free markets" to describe their public purpose, although "free competitive markets" are the very last

thing the Republicans would like to see government pursue.

For Republicans, individuals are bothersome.

They get in the way. They are generally stupid, what with all their prattle about land use plans, limiting abortions, protests over corporate eminent domain and their whining about the power of multinational corporations to extract tax concessions from other citizens in exchange for the location of branch operations.

The end result of the Republican pursuit of this public purpose is a type of multinational corporate tyranny at the Federal level.

The longer the Republicans are in positions of elected power at the Federal level, the closer this end state corporate tyranny comes to reality.

The corporate tyranny is due to the fact that American citizens have no recourse to hold the unelected corporations politically accountable.

The odd consequence of this set of conditions is the Republican advocacy of some type of global governing council on international trade controlled by the largest corporations, and the de-emphasis on the importance of national sovereignty.

The two party system, in America today, is not capable of addressing the issue of the loss of individual and national sovereignty to the trans-national corporations.

Madison's scheme was delivered in the form of a social contract wherein Madison promised that his checks and balances would effectively eliminate control of government by special interests at the state level.

Madison's scheme of politics has eventually evolved into a type of centralized special interest tyranny that subjugates individual freedom to the collective interests of the elite, no matter which political party is in control.

Because Madison's rules of procedure insulated the elites from the will of the citizens so effectively, citizens today have precious little political leverage to regain control of the system.

Through time, the American system of special interest elitism in politics has led to a condition where the social and political elites in Washington, D. C., operate in a nearly closed decision making system, whose rules of participation and procedures the elites control.

As time goes on, the decisions made in Washington seem to be more and more disconnected from the consent of the citizens, and beyond their control to participate in it, even in the most limited form of fair elections for electing the elites who will rule them.

In 1787, the common citizens gave up their sovereign rights, without extracting equal rights for all and special privileges for none.

Finding a replacement for the elite self-interest political system is complicated by the evidence that a certain component of elite self interest seems to be exactly the right human motivation for making the competitive market system work.

Hamilton's concern about whether the wealthy would continue to perform their valuable function of making investments in the young economy was not misplaced.

Much of the economic experience and theory in the past 250 years has shown that the increase in social welfare in a future period depends upon keeping the flow of investment capital strong in the current period of time.

Free, competitive, markets, in actual real life, are an essential component of a just political system.

The dilemma of how to keep wealthy people politically happy so that they will continue to make investments has become especially complicated since Adam Smith noted that the self interest of each individual in a competitive market leads to the greatest wealth in society, thus providing the logical basis for concluding that elite economic self interest of wealthy people serves the public purpose.

Madison concluded that the self-interest of the wealthy was a greater good in serving the public purpose than the self-interest of common citizens to participate in a fair political system of equal rights and equal privileges.

Madison's solution for keeping the wealthy happy was to provide a mix of powers in which the wealthy could have their very own branch of government.

The other branches of government must also be kept safely in the hands of the natural aristocracy, with one branch completely insulated by the popular will, but with the constitutional power of the U. S. Supreme Court to override the will as it was expressed either in the state legislatures or the U. S. Congress.

As Elisha Douglass pointed out in Rebels and Democrats, Whig leaders like North Carolina's Sam Johnston understood that the problem for the new constitution was,

"...how to establish a check on the representatives of the people." (Douglass, Elisha P., Rebels and Democrats: The

Struggle for Equal Political Rights and Majority Rule During the American Revolution, University of North Carolina Press, 1955.).

Once the barriers against democracy were established, just like the Leviathan, Madison's original constitutional check on common citizens was irrevocable.

Few, if any of Madison's cohorts worried about the basic contradiction unleashed by their constitutional scheme.

As Douglass noted,

"Hence, a double paradox: to preserve their own liberty, the unprivileged masses must be prevented from infringing on the privileged few; to maintain a government based on consent, a large proportion of the people must be deprived of the ability to extend or withhold consent."

This logic of elite rule served the slaveocracy well, under the Whigs, the Federalists and the Democrats, for many years.

As the old slave trader John C. Calhoun noted, the basic units of politics in America were aggregations of whole interests and classes, not individuals.

In all of his resolutions introduced in Congress, and in all of his political advocacy on behalf of the slaveocracy, the society Calhoun advocated consisted of two pillars, the white slave owners and the white property owners, with white non-property owners excluded from political participation.

"Only the slaveholders," said Calhoun, quoted in the Wilenz book,

"had the intelligence and the will, as well as the material interests to resist this hegemony of democratic majority rule."

Thomas Jefferson captured the essence of how to resolve this contradiction between property rights and political rights in the American political tradition.

In the political realm, Jefferson suggested that the goal of the constitutional set up should be a civil society,

"where no man should do against his will the bidding of another."

In the economic realm, Jefferson advocated a society,

"where no man was so poor as to be forced to sell himself, and none so rich as to be able to buy him."

Jefferson's solution has never been implemented. But, his ideas form the basis of the American democratic impulse.

He clearly understood that democracy was a form of political participation, and that the constitution should have been the document that preserved and protected the rights of citizens, not the synthetic social class interests of the ruling class and the members of the Southern slaveocracy.

The purpose of this book is to re-examine the legacy of America's democratic impulse of fair political participation, and to explore the question of the relationship between the pursuit of individual self interest, free market economics, and the constitutional public purpose of individual liberty.

In other words, the intent of this book is to advocate the implementation of Jefferson's ideals in practice, in a new constitution that re-starts the American experiment from its Spirit of Liberty, anti-federalists roots.

The new constitution described in this book provides an alternative to Madison's exclusion of citizens from the deliberations of government.

The reforms are based upon Jefferson's notion that those who would be bound by laws should have the greatest say in making the laws, and his insight that that those who make their own laws and rules would adhere to them.

It does not matter how widely dispersed or balanced Madison's special interests may be if the constitutional public purpose of equal political rights is not made as the explicit goal of the constitution.

Madison did not foresee the case where American corporate citizens would operate outside of the territory of the nation, to the economic detriment of the nation.

Or, the even more unbelievable case where U. S. Supreme Court Justices look to foreign laws and international treaties to interpret U. S. Constitutional questions.

Madison did not foresee that a common Marxist ideology, held by all branches of government, and all the staff who work in government agencies, would replace his system of institutional checks and balance of commercial factions with a totalitarian ideology.

Obligation to serve the public purpose, as offered by Jefferson, is derived from the recognition of reciprocal advantage in achieving individual independence, which is obtained from social cooperation in civil rule making and rule enforcement.

Each individual citizen is assumed to have the capacity to see the self-evident truth of the reciprocal advantage to be gained through cooperation.

The new constitution advocated in this book is based upon Jefferson's faith in citizens that reciprocity in political authority is based upon an exchange of trust that citizens will honor the claims and rights of others.

On any matter of public policy or a question of discerning the public purpose, the reforms contained in this book pose the question:

"What promotes the greatest degree of individual liberty to control decisions over the individual's own life time choices?"

The social glue that holds dissociated individuals together in this political system is the recognition by each individual that the advantages gained through politically equal cooperation for each individual are greater than the benefits currently derived from America's dysfunctional political system of unequal rights.

The rules of political cooperation developed through the process of reciprocal exchange of trust continually bind the individual to the system of authority because the individual can imagine that political rules and rights could easily be reversed, or worse yet, be dictated by a self-interested political elite.

In Constitutional Economics, James Buchanan wrote that,

"Uncertainty about where one's own interest will lie in a sequence of plays or rounds will lead a rational person, from his own self-interest, to prefer rules and arrangements, or constitutions, that will seem fair, no matter what final positions he might occupy." (Buchanan, James M., Constitutional Economics, Blackwell, 1991.).

The two essential conditions for Buchanan's constitutional system to work are the belief that individuals pursue their rational self-interest, and that the constitution identifies the pursuit of the rational self-interest as the goal of a democratic republic.

The pathway out of the current dysfunctional two party system is an entirely new constitution that equips citizen's with more structural power to defend their own interests against either unelected government power, or the unauthorized power of non-elected corporations whose behavior is in no way accountable to citizens.

Madison's and Hamilton's flaw, while not an optimal constitutional system in the earlier history, at least provided long periods of political stability, interrupted about every 10 years by economic and financial collapse.

Special interest corruption served an important political purpose of binding ruling class elites from both political parties to the nation's financial interest.

With the shift to the global international control over technological innovation and economic growth of multinational elites, the flaw in the constitution becomes lethal to the interests of common citizens domiciled in the 50 states.

The choice in America today is between greater collectivism and more centralized power in the hands of global corporations, or greater power in the hands of individual citizens, at the state level of government.

This book is about how to reclaim the democratic impulse in order to move forward on the second alternative.

Chapter 2. The Origins of Madison's British Social Class Anti-Individualism.

Madison faced a dilemma as he prepared to replace the Articles of Confederation.

Madison understood, according to Marvin Meyers, in The Mind of the Founder, that man was a "social" animal moved by self-interest. (Meyers, Marvin, The Mind of the Founder: Sources of the Political Thought of James Madison, University Press of New England, 1981.).

Madison's dilemma was how to re-write the rules of the Articles of Confederation so that,

"...self-interested, self-governing men would be obliged to respect the rights of others and serve the permanent and aggregate interests of the community."

Whenever Madison refers to "self-interested, self-governing men," he means the American natural aristocracy, because only the wealthy elites had the moral quality of virtue.

Madison's model of society was the British social class conflict model, where the

American natural aristocracy functioned like the British lords.

Our argument is that the revolution of 1776 was fought to throw off the British social class system in order to implement a revolutionary philosophy of individualism.

Madison staged a counter-revolution in 1787, to re-impose the British social class structure in America.

Madison's dilemma of how to make the American ruling class serve the "aggregate community interests," was never successfully solved because his rules left out the definition in his Preamble of the public purpose to be served by government.

Madison's rules were based upon the financial competition between social classes, not on the protection of individual liberty.

We argue that in order to reclaim the American democratic impulse, it is necessary to go back in history to determine what the original intent of the Revolution of 1776 was, and how Madison derived his anti-individualist philosophy of government.

In mulling over how to solve his dilemma, Madison drew upon the works of many philosophers before him, among them Thomas Hobbes, Edmund Burke, and John Locke.

When Thomas Hobbes was writing The Leviathan, in the late 1640s, he had two earlier patterns of social authority to use as examples in developing his own model of civil authority. (Hobbes, Thomas, Leviathan, London, J.M. Dent & Sons, Ltd, [n.d.].).

Those two patterns of authority had coexisted for many years, and each had been undergoing a slow transformation, the outcome of which fascinated Hobbes.

Hobbes was writing about what social order would replace either the King or the Church in performing the social function of holding dissociated individuals together in a cooperative society, and what force would compel the ruler's obligation to serve the public purpose.

This was the same question Madison faced in his effort to replace the Articles of Confederation.

One pattern of social authority existed before the time of Jesus.

In his work, The Historical Jesus, John Crossan describes this early pattern as patriarchic clientage. (Crossan, John Dominic, The Historical Jesus: The Life of a Mediterranean Jewish Peasant, 1st ed., Harper, 1991.).

In this social authority pattern, individuals owed allegiance to their elite, or patriarch.

The fundamental question of obligation to society raised by Hobbes was solved in patriarchic clientage at birth.

Individuals were born into existing clientage relationships.

Relationships could change over an individual's life, generally as a result of some cataclysmic event like war or famine, but most likely, the existing pattern would endure from generation to generation.

Any single individual would be subjected to the will of the patriarch, who would compel obligation to serve the public purpose, which was synonymous with faithfully serving the patriarch.

When individuals who served the same elite were grouped together, the individuals tended to have some defining characteristics in common.

Some of the defining characteristics had to do with the individual's religion, or with the geographical place of birth, or with the craft or occupation of the individual.

These common characteristics of the group were important to Hobbes when he looked back at the authority pattern of patriarchic clientage and developed his ideas of social collectives and social obligation.

Eventually, the characteristics of the group became a more important variable in Hobbes' model of civil authority than the welfare of the individuals themselves.

Part of the modern day tangle of values between individual rights and social authority relates to this early emphasis of groups, as a unit of analysis in sociological inquiry, as opposed to the use of the individual, as the primary unit of analysis.

Social order, under patriarchic clientage, was maintained over long periods because the different patriarchs cooperated with each other on certain social customs and unwritten rules.

This type of cooperation among elites tended to keep the social pattern in force.

Crossan provides, as an example of cooperation among elites, the trial of Jesus, where Jewish elites took Jesus to Roman civil elites for trial as a result of obedience to patriarchic social rules.

Social unrest, like the great Jewish uprisings in 50 A.D., were the result of failure of patriarchs to reciprocate and cooperate in observing social customs and rules.

This failure to reciprocate in deference to existing social customs also caused unrest between individual clients and their patriarch, when the clients failed to provide the proper measure of value in an exchange with their elite.

Reciprocation acted as a type of social rule enforcement mechanism that allowed for social stability, when rules were followed.

The terms of exchange, or the quality of values being exchanged in observing the social rules of reciprocity, were set primarily by the position of social authority the individual occupied.

The model of exchange in relationships is important to a particular type of political inquiry called " constitutional contract" theory, where social interaction is assumed to be patterned on individuals entering hypothetical contracts.

Hobbes, and later, Locke, were philosophers who used the model of a hypothetical contract to explain why individuals would leave a state of nature to enter a civil constitutional contract.

In the ancient tradition of patriarchic exchange, reciprocation did not require some measure of equality of values being exchanged.

The values to be exchanged were established by social custom, and were based upon the widely accepted view that certain individuals did not possess the mental attributes required to judge the level of values required for any exchange.

The view that certain individuals were deficient mentally to make decisions meant that reciprocation could not be left to chance or uncertainty in the values being exchanged.

For whatever value that was being exchanged, be it loyalty, respect, honor, faith, or money, the terms and conditions of exchange were known by each party prior to the exchange, and had been established long before by social rules and conventions.

Failure to reciprocate in this social context meant not following the rules of exchange.

Not following the rules of exchange meant not serving the patriarch, which meant not discharging the obligation to serve the public purpose.

Sometime after the death of Jesus, a second pattern of social authority began to evolve.

Paul Tillich describes some of the ideology of this second authority pattern in his book, A History of Christian Thought. (Tillich, Paul, A History of Christian Thought: From Is Judaic and Hellenistic Origins to Existentialism, Simon and Schuster, 1972.).

Throughout the book, Tillich contrasts the philosophical views of Christian thinkers with the actual institutional authority pattern of the Christian Church.

This contrast is particularly revealing because the philosophies expressed by the Christian thinkers, and the actual exercise of authority of the institutional Church were so different.

The contrast provided a dilemma for Hobbes, and other social philosophers, in the investigation of social authority patterns.

Should they focus on what the church philosophers said, or should they emphasize what the Church actually did, with regard to the exercise of authority?

As an example of this dilemma, the question of whether any individual had the mental capacity to make judgments about the level of exchange of faith required in serving God is useful.

Some Christian thinkers reasoned that because humans are made in the image of God, that they contained the innate ability to reciprocate directly with God in the discharge of their faith.

In actual practice of authority, the Church determined that individuals were not capable of serving God without the mediation of the Church.

The obligation of an individual to serve God, and, as a consequence, to serve the public purpose, was too important to leave the proper exchange of values to chance.

In this church authority pattern, serving God was synonymous with serving the public purpose.

The rules of reciprocation in the exchange of faith in the Church involved three actors: the Church, as an institution of authority, the individual, and God.

The Church saw individuals as owing an obligation to obey the Church in order to discharge their obligation to serve God.

Any single individual was subjugated to the will of God in this tri-part exchange, which first meant being subjugated to the will of the Church, through its sovereign on earth.

Like the earlier authority pattern of patriarchic clientage, the authority pattern of the Church involved elites, arranged in a hierarchy of power, and non-elites, who shared certain characteristics in common.

The duration and stability of the pattern of authority in the Church, however, did not depend so much on elite cooperation as in the case of patriarchic clientage.

Authority and social order in the Church was maintained by strict obedience to the will of the Sovereign on earth, by all of the subordinate, underling elites.

This example of strict obedience to the sovereign on earth became an important component of order in Hobbes' pattern of civil authority.

Hobbes' borrowed elements of the group characteristics of individuals from patriarchic clientage and the example of a sovereign on earth from the Church as important components of deriving obligation to serve the public purpose.

The reciprocity in the exchange of faith in the Church involved a complicated three way process.

In the first part of the exchange, God says what his will is, and the Church acts as the interpreter of God's word.

The Church then turns to each grouping of individuals, and tells each grouping what God has said.

Upon hearing this command, each individual in the group acts out his life in accordance with faith.

Upon the execution of a lifetime of the exchange of faith, the individual is rewarded by God's reciprocation of faith by entering the eternal kingdom of heaven.

This process of reciprocation in the exchange of faith seems oddly unidirectional.

The currency, or medium of exchange, is faith.

In exchange of an individual's lifetime of faith in God, God reciprocates.

Jack Miles, in his book, God: A Biography, noted how odd he thought this process must seem to God. (Miles, Jack, God: A Biography, 1st ed., Alfred A. Knopf, 1995.).

The Church sets God up to be an all-powerful Being, whose words command a lifetime of faith.

What God says affects the behavior of individuals throughout their lives.

Yet, the affect on God on what the individuals are doing never seems to matter very much in the authority pattern of the Church.

Miles suggests that this lack of affect on God may be one reason why God stops making appearances in the Bible, and has fallen strangely silent for the past several thousand years.

Like the exchanges in patriarchic clientage, the parties to the exchanges in the Church knew in advance the terms and conditions of the exchange.

This certain knowledge was necessary because the pattern of authority in the Church assumed that individuals did not possess the mental attributes to judge, on their own, what level of faith was required to be exchanged.

However, unlike the earlier pattern of authority, in the Church, the value of the exchange to one party, namely God, is never questioned or defined by the Church.

The two patterns of authority, clientage and the Church, coexisted for many years, and drew support from each other.

In other words, the two patterns of authority tended to compliment each other because so many of their features were similar.

One of the important similarities between the two authority patterns was the commonly-held belief that people in certain social classes were incapable of making judgments about social rules of obligation and reciprocity.

All of these patterns contain some common features regarding the treatment and definition of individuals.

Each pattern has some notion or conception of obligation and reciprocation in the social exchanges that promote the public purpose.

Hobbes stood at the threshold in time of the two older authority patterns looking back in history, and the two newer authority patterns looking forward.

Hobbes was trying to come up with the solution to the problem he saw in the newer authority patterns, not yet developed, but at least discernable, of how dissociated individuals would be bound together in a cooperative society.

Hobbes initially assumed that the key feature of all human societies was the biological urge of any individual to subjugate other individuals, in other words, to seek power over another.

Hobbes also assumed that the primary public purpose of binding individuals together in a cooperative society was the maintenance of social order.

According to C. B. Macpherson, in The Political Theory of Possessive Individualism, what Hobbes sought to develop in his hypothetical model of society were methods and procedures that provided for peaceful, nonviolent ways for men to seek power over others. (Macpherson, C.B., The Political Theory of Possessive Individualism: Hobbes to Locke, Wynford Books, 2011.).

Hobbes' definition of the public purpose is important because it tends to act as a historical reference point for subsequent philosophers in their thinking about the public purpose, and eventually informed Madison on the issue of how the natural aristocracy in America would serve the public purpose.

Hobbes thought that it would be useful to include certain biological features of humans in the development of a formula for pursuing the socially acceptable public purpose of maintaining social order.

This combination would be consistent with the emerging "natural philosophy and natural rights" doctrines being developed across many social and scientific endeavors in Europe.

The two primary biological features that Hobbes chose to emphasize were the urge to subjugate, and the lack of mental capacity of some individuals to make decisions either about their own welfare or that of society.

The ability of an individual to define and pursue self-interest has subsequently become the key variable in explaining the development of social authority patterns since the time of Hobbes.

The variable of an individual's capacity to pursue self interest provides a convenient method of distinguishing between the sociological inquiry of socialist collectivist authority patterns that use groups as the primary unit of analysis, or an inquiry that assumes the individual to be the primary unit of analysis.

The use of groups tends to lead to more collectivistic solutions, wherein elites make decisions about what is in the best interests of society, while the use of individuals as the primary unit of analysis leads more to inquiry like the one Jefferson had in mind in his writing of the Declaration of Independence.

In the collectivist socialist authority pattern, control over the aggregations of individuals, based upon some type of defining characteristics, become more important to maintaining social order than the welfare of any single individual.

In socialist philosophy, individuals are aggregated into groups, under a collectivist authority pattern, and decisions about the welfare of the group as a whole, are made by an elite, on behalf of the group.

The individuals in the group accept their group identification as the primary definition of who they are as individuals.

In contrast to collectivism, the social authority patterns of individualism assume that each individual is capable of making decisions about the individual's self-interest.

The ability of any human to make decisions about self- interest was assumed by Jefferson to be a biologically self-evident observable fact.

The individual's identity is not first and foremost defined by the group or tribe, but through the mental process of imagining the individual's own identity and taking the further mental step of imagining the identity of another individual.

The public purpose of maintaining social order in the individualist authority pattern is tempered by the equally important public purpose of defining social rules of cooperation allowing for each individual to define and pursue self-interest.

No elite is assumed to have a greater ability or authority to make decisions on behalf of the welfare of either the individual or aggregations of individuals.

Hobbes wrestled with these biologically observable facts in his attempt to reconcile self-interest with obligation to society.

He finally related self-interest to what he called the desire for an individual to maintain motion.

On the one hand, Hobbes could see a type of equality in each individual's wants, and rights, and the ability of each individual to make decisions about pursuing those interests.

On the other hand, the two earlier social authority patterns he drew from assumed that a few selected individuals were superior in making decisions about individual and social welfare.

Hobbes then set about to define how these few individuals were "selected."

Hobbes reached his resolution after developing a method of inquiry in which he imagined a hypothetical state of society called "state of nature."

In the state of nature, imaginary civilized men, who were contemporaries with Hobbes in terms of education and morals, would be placed in a completely unorganized society to see what kind of rules of cooperation they would develop.

In this imaginary state of nature, Hobbes assumed that neither of the two earlier authority patterns were operative.

Hobbes then asked the question of what force would obligate any single individual to follow or obey the social rules that had been developed after they had left the state of nature.

Hobbes came up with a set of rules on reciprocation in social exchange between individuals.

His imaginary rules and society looked very much like what has come to be called a "free market" exchange society.

The reciprocation occurred in a hypothetical market place that the civilized men had agreed to create when they left the state of nature.

This marketplace society would allow individuals to peacefully seek power over others.

In the initial stages of this market society, each individual's urge to seek power over another was equal, as well as the ability of each individual to discern what was in that individual's best self-interest.

It was this original characterization of equal power in exchange relationships promoted by Hobbes that has contributed much to the tangle of American economic values about free market exchange and the political values of natural individual rights.

Subsequent generations of social philosophers have confused and conjoined the role of power in how individual's pursue self-interest in the market, and the role of rights as political values, which should lead to rules of justice about how individuals discharge their obligation to society.

Hobbes rejected the notion that an individual's obligation to follow social rules in this market society could be established by reference to doing God's work on earth.

He also rejected the authority pattern of patriarchic clientage, with the example of elites cooperating with each other to maintain social order.

In the hypothetical market exchange society created by Hobbes, all values and rights were established by the operation of the market place, where individuals sought power over others.

Having rejected God as a power to compel obedience to the rules of the market, Hobbes came up with the closest approximation of the God in heaven, by creating a God on earth.

Hobbes called his earthly God "Leviathan."

Leviathan had awful, awesome powers to compel obligation to follow the social rules that civilized men had agreed upon, when they left the state of nature.

Further, once individuals agreed to leave the state of nature to enter the market society, in the initial social contract, Leviathan would be perpetual.

Leviathan could never be removed or challenged. His authority was absolute and irrevocable.

Hobbes reduced all of society to exchanges between individuals in a market, whose currency was power.

In place of moral principals guiding individual behavior, Hobbes substituted market exchange.

The market became God, and all morality and obligation was the morality of the market.

This view of morality influenced Madison's thinking about modern contemporary obligation of the natural aristocracy to serve the public purpose because he assumed that only the natural aristocracy possessed the moral value of virtue.

Hobbes postulated a certain type of equality, which sounds good to modern ears, and then went on to describe a despotic society that subjugated the sovereignty of the individual to the sovereignty of the market.

The sovereignty of the market has the power of God, and an ideology associated with the benefits of the free market system continues to draw legitimacy and sustenance from a set of social values that are nominally democratic.

Those few individuals who possessed the greatest market power were the ones "selected" by Hobbes to make decisions about society on behalf of all other citizens.

The contemporary interpretation of this concept is that the wealthy are possessed of special powers based upon the observable fact that they are wealthy, in the market.

There is no concept of distributive justice in this society, because the concept of justice is limited to what can be obtained in market exchanges.

There is only exchange justice in this society, and the currency of exchange is power.

As pointed out by MacPherson, in Hobbes' world, justice is simply a commodity in a market of transactions based upon the currency of power.

For Hobbes, what replaced the Church or the King in compelling obligation to serve the public purpose was the market.

What compels obligation in the market is Leviathan, a type of God on earth.

What started out in Hobbes as a fairly promising exercise of seeing what civilized men would do in a state of nature resulted in a set of rules as authoritarian collectivist as the two earlier patterns of authority.

Elements of the pattern of authority that Hobbes imagined in his book were important as historical reference points for Madison.

Hobbes, however, did not provide the complete logical justification for his system, leaving Madison with important gaps to fill.

The philosophical linchpin between Hobbes and Madison was provided by John Locke, who had the benefit of more years of observation than Hobbes about what was occurring during the mid 1600s.

Locke could more clearly see that the Industrial Revolution had created a new social actor, who placed self interest above the demands of the Church, kin, or community. (Locke, John, The Second Treatise of Government: An Essay Concerning the True Original, Extent and End of Civil Government, and A Letter Concerning Toleration, edited by Charles L. Sherman, Irvington, 1979.).

For Locke, the main motivation of this new social actor were the goals of upward occupational mobility and self improvement.

Locke moved these two motivations to the center of his moral universe.

Like Hobbes, Locke started out with some general observations on certain types of equality between individuals.

Locke first noted that all individuals were equal in their ownership of their own human capital, which Locke called human labor.

From this initial premise of equality, Locke went a step further to suggest that individual ownership of human capital implied an equal right to own other types of capital, loosely identified by Locke as "property."

Locke then reasoned that if individuals had an equal right to own property, that they also had a right to accumulate any property with which they had mixed their own labor.

Locke then applied another logical connection that if individuals had the right to accumulate property, they also had a right to accumulate an unlimited amount of property.

Like Hobbes' imaginary agreement that men agreed to create the market society when they left the state of nature, Locke also proposed an imaginary agreement between individuals about unlimited property accumulation.

Locke suggested that the widespread imaginary agreement to use money as a common unit of value for market exchanges meant that individuals had agreed to unequal, unlimited, accumulation of property.

Up to this point in Locke's pattern of moral social authority, nothing about the unlimited accumulation of property in economic market exchanges affected the distribution of political rights in Locke's proposed civil society.

Locke had started out with some observations about equality among individuals, and an unstated, unwritten assumption about human nature, that all rational individuals shared aspirations for upward occupational mobility and property accumulation.

Locke's unwritten assumption about human nature applied to the emerging market industrial society that Locke could see developing.

Locke's unwritten assumption about shared aspirations for upward occupational mobility and property accumulation has contributed mightily to the tangled confusion of American values between political rights and economic self-interest.

On the one hand, Locke's notion of equal shared aspirations represented a break with tradition that certain individuals had brains which were biologically deficient to make decisions about their own welfare.

On the other side, Locke replaced biological deficiency with a psychological deficiency that tended to have the same outcome on individual sovereignty.

Locke suggested that those individuals who did not share in this aspiration for unlimited property accumulation were irrational.

Being irrational, the individuals were not qualified to participate in collective political decisions.

It was at this juncture of applying Locke's thinking to the American constitution that Madison's conception of political values became tangled with values derived from economic exchanges motivated by rational self interest in the market place.

An individual attribute, observed in market behavior, was linked to the pattern of rights in the constitutional political system created by Madison.

Madison understood this connection, and Hamilton was obsessed with this relationship.

Locke created a division in society between those individuals who were rational, as seen by the shared desire for upward occupational mobility, and those who were seen as irrational, by virtue of the fact that they did not, or had not, accumulated property.

Irrational people, reasoned Locke, were not qualified to make political decisions, and did not possess the required attributes that would confer equal political rights in the civil society created when individuals left the state of nature.

In the historical progression of Locke's thinking about social authority patterns, the right of property came first, in a pre-civil society, similar to Hobbes' state of nature.

After the right of property had been established, the next event in Locke's thinking was an imaginary agreement by individuals to use money as the medium of exchange for property transactions.

The quantity of money possessed by any individual became an observed verification of the rationality of the individual.

The next event, according to Locke, was the establishment of civil society, whose major job was to protect the property that had been accumulated from expropriation by the King, the institutional Christian Church, or by the newest entrant to the pattern of social authority, which Locke called the State.

In a process of delegation of authority similar to the one Hobbes' had in mind when individuals created Leviathan, Locke said that men delegated authority to the State to protect property.

The act of delegation was binding on all generations, and was the primary force that compelled continuing obligation of individuals to serve the public purpose.

Once delegated, in the initial grant of authority that created the social contract, the authority given to the State could not be revoked.

The public purpose would be served, according to Locke, by providing property owners what they needed in the way of social authority, which in Madison, became the use of the police power of the state to protect property from mal-appropriation by the property-less common citizens.

Part of public purpose was served by rules that allowed individuals to accumulate unlimited amounts of property and part of the purpose of government was to protect private property.

Human labor, which started out in Locke's thinking as a common element of equality among individuals, became simply another commodity to be exchanged in the market.

Since labor, once stripped of its humanity, and then exchanged in the market as a commodity, was not rational, it could not be allowed to participate in either decisions about its own welfare or the welfare of society.

In Locke's pattern of civil authority, labor had no discernable self-interest because it did not possess the human motivation to accumulate property.

The only property labor possessed was that with which it was born, and labor agreed to part with that property for the agreed upon unit of value, money.

Labor was a thing to be exchanged in the market.

From the perspective of the Locke's property rights, labor simply existed as a thing to be managed in the pursuit of the public purpose.

According to C. B. MacPherson,

"It was not that the interests of the laboring class were subordinated to the national interest. The laboring class was not considered to have an interest; the only interest was the ruling-class view of the national interest."

Once again, a theoretical justification for a social authority pattern was emerging, in the Industrial Revolution, which denied that certain individuals were capable of making decisions about their own self-interest, or the public interest.

In the earlier patterns of patriarchic clientage, and the institutional Christian Church, the denial was based upon a widely-shared belief that some human brains were biologically deficient to independently comprehend the mechanics of the exchange of faith.

In the later interpretations of this phenomena given by Locke, the denial was based more on a psychological deficiency associated with lack of motivation to accumulate property, which logically implied a lack of capacity to make rational decisions.

The outcome, for both patterns of social authority however, was the same type of collectivist authoritarianism of elite rule.

What emerged in all cases was a justification for a type of social collectivism, in which elites made decisions about the welfare of individuals who were lumped together in a social group called "labor."

The newer social authority patterns of property accumulation in the market and the protection of property in the political system supported each other.

Hobbes' God on earth, the Leviathan of the market, drew sustenance from Locke's political theory of the public purpose.

The market, encompassing all ensuing human exchanges, created values and morals.

The values and morals of the market were enforced by the police power of the State, which had received an irrevocable grant of authority when the citizens left the state of nature.

The primary purpose of the State was to protect the existing distribution of property from the social classes who may use the power of government, if they had obtained equal political rights to make political decisions.

Initially, Locke's civil authority pattern looks good to modern eyes because it embraces the principle of making collective decisions by democratic majority rule.

On closer inspection, Locke's interpretation of majority rule contains some important provisos written in very small print at the bottom, and in the margins, of his pages.

One of the important provisos in Locke's pattern of authority was similar to the proviso that compelled obligation in Hobbes' work.

Hobbes wrote that those that made the laws were obligated to follow the laws.

Locke derived his concept of obligation from the delegation of authority that individuals gave to the State in pre-civil society.

Once authority had been delegated to the state, only property owners had any power to make and enforce the laws of the State.

The elites made and enforced social rules which the non-elites were obligated to follow.

Locke wrote that those with the greatest financial interest in the laws should have the greatest say in making the laws.

However, once laws had been made, everyone in Locke's society was bound to follow the laws.

Only the property owners, who had been deemed rational by Locke, could be given power to make laws.

Only property owners had the ability to discern their own self-interest, which entitled them to the exclusive power to interpret the pursuit of the public purpose.

Because the non-property owners were irrational, and did not know what was in their self interest, their self interests had to be treated as a collective public interest of the State.

An example from history shows how this proviso works in practice.

In this nation's only military coup d'etat, the elected city government of Wilmington, N. C. was overthrown in November of 1898, by the former slave-owning elites of the Democratic Party of North Carolina.

The elites were mad because a coalition of republicans and blacks had been elected the majority in the city elections.

In seeking to justify the overthrow, the *Wilmington Semi-Weekly Messenger* wrote:

"Intelligent citizens...owning the greatest percent of the property and paying the greatest percent of the taxes should rule."

This is the general philosophy of Locke, that the property owners should have greater political power than other citizens.

This first proviso, of who is fit to rule, is closely related to a second proviso in Locke's system of civil authority concerning upward occupational mobility.

In this proviso, Locke hit upon a genuinely real biological trait in humans to protect and enhance their economic survival in the newly emerging industrial society.

This proviso plays the same role for Locke that the human biological urge to dominate others plays in Hobbes' work.

In each case, the writers identified a human trait that appears generally universal, and each philosopher applied the trait to the development of their pattern of authority.

In each case, the biological trait tends to bolster the logical appeal of the system of authority being developed by linking something real to something that is imagined.

In Locke's case, the urge to enhance one's economic welfare represented the key variable in determining rationality.

Social status, and political power, for Locke, were not given by place of birth, or by tradition, but by market-based acquisition of property.

The higher an individual's ascent in upward occupational mobility, the more status an individual achieved, as evidenced by their greater ownership of property.

The more status a person achieved, the greater the evidence of rationality and concomitantly, the greater the level of political power granted to the individual under Locke's system of authority.

Something that occurred in the market was linked to something that occurred in the political system.

Social status, and subsequently political power, was achieved through a series of reciprocal exchanges in the market.

The reciprocation for Locke's system was based upon the exchange of money, but either rational party to the exchange could freely determine the appropriate value of money to be exchanged for any single transaction.

Reciprocation in Locke's system did not require a God on earth, or a patriarch, to predetermine the correct level of values to be exchanged, and the absence of the patriarchic rules or God represented a break with the past rules of social reciprocation.

In Locke's system of authority, individuals who are rational can define their own self interest in market exchanges.

Civil society is created and maintained exclusively for the benefit of these rational individuals.

The public purpose is served when individuals accumulate property.

The role of government is to facilitate exchanges by providing an orderly market, keeping the currency stable, and enforcing the terms of any individual legal contract for exchange.

The logical flaw in this second proviso as it relates to the system of authority is the availability of an unlimited supply of property that Locke postulates to exist in pre-civil society.

In pre-civil society, an individual becomes a property owner by mixing the labor of his own human capital with other property.

Locke's entire logical system of authority depends on this supply of property always remaining in abundance, even after civil society has been created.

If there is not an unlimited supply of property, then non-property owners do not have an open path of upward occupational mobility.

If they did not have an open path of mobility, they could never demonstrate the attribute of rationality, and thus gain political rights.

Furthermore, once the rational, property holders were in a position of unchallenged power in the government, they could make rules that guaranteed that the protection of the existing distribution of property became synonymous with serving the public purpose.

Locke's system of political authority tangles up the assumed activities of an individual in market exchanges with post-civil society political rights in a way that creates the conditions for collectivism in a nominally democratic political system.

This has become one of the outcomes of Madison's constitutional scheme.

As a result of Locke's theory, the elite's political self interest in preserving property rights in America has gotten hopelessly tangled up in the distribution of political rights and the development of constitutional rules.

Once the American civil society had been created, elites controlled the development of laws on property exchanges and obtained a perpetual monopoly on determining the public purpose.

Following Locke's theory of political authority, Madison accepted the premise that civil society consisted primarily of an exchange of values in either the economic or the political market.

It did not seem to matter to Madison that the values and instruments in economic exchange may be different than the values in political exchange.

From Madison's point of view, when the proprietors of labor left the state of nature to form the social contract, they agreed that the purpose of the contract was to establish rules governing the exchange relationships, and that the new government must have power to enforce the orderly mechanisms of exchange.

Madison set about to create the constitutional rules that would bring about the orderly exchange mechanism by emphasizing the separation of powers through his system of formal checks and balances.

Because exchange in the early version of America's social contract could easily apply to either market transactions or political exchange, natural rights as a guiding philosophy of the purpose of government was viewed by Madison as morally equivalent in either type of exchange.

His emphasis was on creating constitutional rules of exchange that could be applied by government in a morally neutral environment, where the agencies of government acted like a referee in a football game.

Madison had the benefit of peering back in time to see both Hobbes' and Locke's view of paternalistic clientage as a mode of social organization.

He could see more clearly how the emerging forces of free market exchange influenced social relationships and the social hierarchy of class.

Madison, and more particularly Hamilton, grasped the idea that market exchange was related to both an individual's social standing, and that successful elites played an important role in creating the conditions of economic growth through their investment of capital.

Neither of them seemed to grasp the fundamental difference, explained by C. B. MacPherson, in The Political Theory of Possessive Individualism, that faith and trust in constitutional political exchanges created a shared sense of civic obligation, while market exchanges can be obtained in an orderly manner, without the benefit of faith, trust or moral obligation to serve the public purpose.

From the view point of natural rights, market exchanges are not the moral equivalent of political exchanges, because market exchanges do not create bonds that tie together disassociated individuals in a cooperative society.

Part of Madison's flaw of failing to write the purpose of individual freedom into the Preamble of the constitution is that an orderly system of market exchanges that protects property substitutes special interest greed as the basis of binding individuals to the system of authority, whose major dynamic is competitive special interest exploitation of the rules.

In the analogy of the football game, Madison's constitution created the rules of the financial game, and the enforcement of rules during the game is determined by the Federal judicial referees.

Madison was primarily concerned with rules that would separate powers in a national government to the end that the government, acting as the referee, would be more effective, for protecting the property rights of the wealthy social classes than the rules established by the Articles of Confederation that were primarily concerned with state sovereignty in a national confederation.

The act of creating rules however, and the end to which those rules are directed, what philosophers call the "telos" of the rules, are complementary ingredients needed to bind individuals together in the pursuit of civic interests.

Separation of powers, by itself, does not establish allegiance to follow the rule of law.

James Buchanan addressed this question in his book, The Theory of Public Choice, II, when he described the difference between "economic man," and "moral man." (Buchanan, James M., Theory of Public Choice: Political Applications of Economics, University of Michigan Press, 1972.).

Economic man, according to Buchanan, is defined by his utility function, whose variables are weighted according to their contribution to monetary wealth.

"His behavior," notes Buchanan,

"in the economic relationship is not influenced by ethical or moral considerations that serve to constrain his pursuit of his objectively defined interest."

Buchanan was making the argument in his book that a clean distinction be made between the constitutional rules that govern economic exchanges, and those constitutional rules that define ethical relationships between individuals.

Under one set of constitutional rules, market exchanges are the supreme social values, and investment decisions, which partially determine both prices and justice, are left to the private investment decisions of elites.

The absence of morality in economic exchanges necessitates the deployment of the police power of the state to enforce the terms and conditions of the economic exchange contract.

Under another set of goals, the constitution would create the institutional framework for making collective decisions that did not require dictatorship or police power.

As a result of Madison's failure, the constitutional public purpose means whatever the special interests in control of the U. S. Supreme Court say it means, at the time in history that they happen to be in control.

In Madison's 3-part constitutional scheme of checks and balances, for example, the grid lock between the branches of government that prevents a national consensus on national sovereignty is made worse by any constitutional guidance by the U. S. Supreme Court on what the national purpose is.

This helps to explain why, in the time of Jackson's Democratic Party, the Democrats could legitimately claim that the public purpose was the protection of the weak from the strong, while the Whigs could claim, with equal legitimacy, that the constitutional public purpose was served when government facilitated the development of private financial institutions.

In the absence of Madison writing a constitutional public purpose into his constitution, American political parties, and Supreme Court decisions devolve into special interest squabbling between special interest groups that see a different constitutional public purpose in the constitution.

Any conception of the public purpose is equally valid, because Madison's separation of powers does not address the ends to which that power is directed.

It devolves, in other words, to winning and keeping power.

Allegiance to the rule of law, based upon a shared sense of civic obligation to follow the rules, gives way to rule evasion, based upon the ruse that the constitutional public purpose means something different to each special interest group.

What Madison's careful arrangement of separation of power does is create an effective system of a market exchange society that fails to bind disassociated individuals to a shared sense of civic duty.

In its place, Madison's rules substitute a sense of ruling class shared plunder and greed to exploit the system.

His rules, for example, spell out how slaves should be counted for taxation and voting apportionment decisions, without addressing the larger moral issue of the public purpose served by the market institution of slavery.

Leaving that larger moral issue unsolved, but having rules that address the issue of slaves left the American society with a ticking time bomb that eventually had to be solved on the field of battle.

Madison understood that in the transition from the hypothetical state of nature, before 1776, to civil constitutional society, after 1787, individuals give up some freedoms to gain security through common laws.

In the absence of stating a constitutional telos, his rules had the unfortunate effect of creating a priority of property rights of the natural aristocracy in the constitution over natural rights of individual citizens.

The initial conditions of inequality in property distribution, at the creation of the Constitution in 1787, led to a permanent political inequality in the ensuing civil society.

When property rights are given this priority in rules, then the social function served by free market exchange, which is to provide a vehicle for rational self-interested individuals to pursue their life's mission, does not work.

In entering Madison's constitutional contract, individuals, who were not part of Madison's definition of the natural aristocracy, gave up freedoms without extracting an equal measure of benefits to pursue their sovereignty.

As the southern agrarian populists discovered 100 years later, these guarantees, called the "Bill of Rights," provided an inadequate basis for constitutional reform, given the set of special interests who controlled both rule making and rule enforcement power.

Merrill Peterson, in The Jefferson Image in the American Mind, analyzed the consequences of Madison's flaw, and how it has contributed to the tangle of values between natural rights and the public purpose.

He noted that Madison's division of powers,

"...became the chief means of checking the exaggeration of the democratic principle, and thus of securing an equilibrium of majority power and constitutional guarantees..." (Peterson, Merrill D., The Jefferson Image in the American Mind, Oxford University Press, 1960.).

In other words, Madison's rules became an effective instrument of control precisely because the rules, once adopted, could never be reformed in the direction of more democracy.

More democracy was not a stated "public purpose" of the constitution.

In Madison's constitutional conception, "more democracy" was a bad idea.

In his tour of America in the mid part of the 19th century, de Tocqueville could see more clearly the consequences of Madison's flaw.

He concluded that centralized statism would be the promise of American life, where,

"...a concentration of power and subjection of individuals will increase." (Tocqueville, Alexis de, Democracy in America. The Henry Reeve Text, Vintage Books, 1954.).

Writing from his vantage point in history fifty years before de Tocqueville, John Adams stated that,

"The cohesive powers of "public plunder" will dominate all society. No favors will be attainable but by those who court the ruling demagogues." (The Political Writings of John Adams, 1954.).

In the absence of a constitutional telos, Madison's flaw leaves the task of binding individuals to the public purpose up to the forces of greed through public plunder.

The agents who provide the cohesive force to extract the plunder were never mentioned by Madison in the constitution, but clearly were in his thoughts as he drafted his rules.

The political parties became the machines that kept the special interest system running.

The political parties did not provide the missing ingredients of principles or goals of the system, but the mechanism of power allocation.

As long as all of the separate powers remained safely in the hands of the natural elite, the political parties could provide the cohesive force to coordinate the implementation of those powers across agencies and branches of government.

As they have evolved through time, the two dominant political parties act to screen and filter the right type of candidates into elected office who will continue to distribute the public plunder.

The parties act together to facilitate the orderly, non-violent, means of power transfer from one set of elected officials to the next generation of officials.

And, they act as the mechanism through which local graft and corruption, patronage, and special interests are coordinated with national politics.

In Madison's conception, extending the sphere of political influence across the fruited plain became part of the program where special interest plunder did not have to occur in each of the different localities, it only had to occur in Washington, after the elites arrived in the Capital.

Either political party can lay credible, legitimate claim to representing the best national, public interest, because they each see a different end to the constitution.

In 2020, Madison's political system of operation allowed socialists to capture the levers of power, and fundamentally transform American society into a European collectivist society.

The origins of contemporary American socialist anti-individualism lays within the rules of Madison's constitution with his initial decision that the rules would be based upon social class collectivism, not individualism.

It was a very small philosophical leap for Marxist Democrats to substitute their own concept of collectivism for Madison's ruling class collectivism, once the Marxists gained control of all branches of government, in the election of 2020.

After the Marxists gained unelected, illegitimate authority, Madison's rules had created barriers to constitutional reform so that common natural rights conservatives had no method of amending the constitution, or eliminating the Marxist tyranny.

The first American Revolution was based upon a concept of individual freedom, against the corrupt social class conflict model in England.

Madison's American counter-revolution, in 1787, re-established the British social class conflict model in the Constitution.

The basis of Madison's rules was that common citizens were too irrational to share in government political decisions.

Only the natural aristocracy, who possessed the moral value of virtue, could make and enforce rules.

This same philosophical legacy of anti-individualism in Madison was derived from his understanding of Hobbes and Locke that certain lower social classes were deficient in making decisions about their own self-interest.

Chapter 3. The Agrarian's Lessons of History About Political Reform in America.

About 100 years after the adoption and ratification of the Madison's constitution, the agrarian leader, Tom Watson asked in his newspaper, "What is Labor's Fair Share?"

A better question may have been "What are Fair Rules for Labor to Reform The Constitution?"

The constitutional rules had been set by Madison and Hamilton to achieve separation of powers in the branches of government, the indirect election of representatives, and judicial review of legislation, all intended to bury any incipient tendencies to a popular citizen's democratic government.

In Federalist #39, Madison argued for a new sort of representative republic. It would rest on the,

"total exclusion of the people, in their collective capacity, from any share in government."

Hamilton wrote at the time that he considered the "people as a great beast, howling masses, not fit to govern."

Madison further explained in Federalist #51,

"In framing a government of men over men, one must first empower the government to control the people, and then oblige it (the government) to control itself."

While Madison was successful in creating a government that controlled the people, he was deliberately unsuccessful in establishing rules to allow either the people, or the government, to control itself.

We use the experience of the Agrarian Populist movement, in the 35 years after he Civil War, to demonstrate the impossibility of conventional methods of political reform under Madison's rules.

We could have as easily chosen other politically dispossessed social groups in America, such as Black people after the Civil War, or Native American Indians, or Chinese immigrants or industrial workers, during the Gilded Age, to demonstrate our argument.

All of these other groups had the same type of barriers, as we described in our recent book, America's Final Revolution (Gabby Press, 2022.).

As the Agrarian Populists discovered in the 1880's, the flaw in Madison's plan is that there are no popular democratic controls over the power of government, and there is no way for common citizens to reform the constitutional rules through the existing two party special interest political system.

It is worthwhile to go back in history and study how the populists reached their conclusions about the impossibility of reform, and what happened to them when they attempted political reform.

The Federalist ideology of fearing the citizens contained an assumption that special interest activity would always be based upon the competing actions of special financial interests in diverse geographical areas.

In their set up, the interaction of many different individual commercial private interests would produce a government of common good.

What happened instead is that private special interests across the nation became group special interests, and those group interests formed political coalitions that captured the reins of a powerful central government.

The irony of history is that the Federalist ideology of freedom was supposed to lead to a "common good," but actually led to a collectivist group-oriented, special interest political system.

As Calhoun put many years later, the slaves had to continue to be slaves, after the Civil War, in order for the plantation elite to be free.

What the Agrarian Populists were searching for was a combination of Jefferson's earlier ideologies that would combine authority by the consent of the governed, achieved through citizen participation in government rule decision making, with fair rules of economic exchange.

Through their efforts at economic cooperatives and mass citizen educational meetings, they came to an understanding that their individual self-interests, as farmers, could be improved through a civil society that made the farmer's pursuit of self-interest easier to obtain.

In the mid 1880's, the farmers recognized that the Constitution had trapped them in a type of neo-slavery debt peonage system, with no way to escape.

According to McMath, in Populist Vanguard,

"Alliance leader and many farmers strongly believed the source of their problems to be the credit and marketing system of the cotton culture in which the furnishing merchant loomed as the principal villain."

So, the Agrarian Populists first started out trying to reform the banking and marketing rules of Madison's system.

As their first economic policy response, the leaders of the Alliance created a cooperative exchange network to both provide credit to farmers and market their crops.

As described by Sydney Nathans, in The Quest for Progress, the farmers soon found themselves,

"...clashing head-on with bankers, merchants, railroads and warehousemen, none eager to sacrifice their profits to the cooperative competitors. ...Credit and the currency supply of the entire nation, it became evident, were in the viselike grip of the county's largest bankers, who, in the name of "sound currency" had dictated two decades of deflation and tight money."

The tight money was financially rewarding for bond-holders, but absolutely economic death on farm prices for farmers trying to escape debt peonage.

In addition, as the tight monetary system caused a shortage of liquid cash, which was required for the payment of property taxes, farmers began to lose title to their land because they could not pay their taxes in cash.

The monetary policy had the effect of assisting the political coalition of bankers and furnishing merchants in legal judicial schemes to obtain title to the land of the small landholders.

The dual effect was a greater concentration of land ownership, in the hands of wealthy families, and greater number of formerly free-holders forced into the debt-peonage system.

As described by C. Vann Woodward, in Origins of The New South,

"In their attack on the national banking system, the agrarian economists were on solid ground in contending that private privilege was exercising a sovereign power, a power of regulating national currency, for private gain rather than for meeting the needs of the country."

A private special interest, exercising a sovereign political power to take private property from farmers, however, is the logical outcome of Madison's social class conflict constitutional system.

As a second economic policy response, the Populists developed their sub-treasury plan, which Gavin Wright described as a system of warehouses and elevators that would accept crops from farmers and issue notes equal to 80% of the crop's expected market value.

As a way out of the political vise grip exercised by bankers and merchants, the Populists were trying to replace the tight money, high interest crop mortgage system of debt peonage with a plan that mortgaged the crop to the federal government at low interest.

In other words, they were trying to follow Hamilton's advice about the blessings of debt, but this time, for themselves, not the elite bond holders who had financed the Civil War.

It was an excellent idea, and their reform ideas became the basis for many of the New Deal agricultural programs in the 1930's. However, it did little to help the farmers during the late 1880's.

The farmers relied upon the Democratic Party to implement their sub-treasury plan, primarily through the good offices of U. S. Senator Zeb Vance, Democrat, of North Carolina.

After watching the slow progress of the sub-treasury plan over a period of 10 years in Congress, the farmers became agitated.

In July of 1890, one tenant farmer wrote to Senator Vance, saying

"My Dear Sir, we have been voting with the Democratic Party for the last quarter of a century looking for the relief promised from year to year by our party leaders and find none. We feel, Sir, that we have been deceived and we have become dissatisfied with those who make promises only to be broken."

The inaction of the national Democratic Party in not serving the needs of farmers was mirrored by the activity of the Democratic Party at the state level.

During the late 1880's, the great Populist leader, Leonidas Polk, had been successful in establishing a state agricultural agency in North Carolina.

It had been created with the votes of both Democrats and farm-oriented Republicans.

Soon thereafter, the Democrats achieved control of the General Assembly and cut the funding for the agency, citing the high cost of operation of its 3 person staff, which included Polk, as the first commissioner.

As the first two policy efforts were in the process of failing to deliver relief for the farmers, the leadership of the agrarian movement debated moving in the direction of forming their own political party.

Lawrence Goodwyn, in Democratic Promise, wrote that by the last of the 1880's, the agrarian leaders had seen in both political parties,

"...abundant evidence that great aggregations of capital could cloak self interested policies in high moral purposes, and have such interpretations disseminated widely and persuasively through the nation's press...convincing the leaders of the need for a new political party free of corporate control."

The strategy to move the Agrarian Populists into politics, and to create a third political party, was contentious and divisive issue, causing a split between the leadership of the agrarian movement and the common citizen farmer members of the Alliance.

Some historians, among them Michael Schwartz, in Radical Protest and Social Structure, believe that this underlying split between the leaders and the members of the agrarian movement explains why the Populist Party ultimately failed.

"The final option," for the leaders according to Schwartz, was a "massive entry into politics, which ultimately freed the state leadership from its dependency on membership."

The rank and file farmers had achieved economic power in the first two policy efforts, but in the new political party, the members had no power.

There was no relationship between improvement in the farmer's individual financial interest and the political changes that the political system needed to make in order to improve the lives of the farmers.

With the creation of the new political party, according to Schwartz,

"The oligarchization of the Alliance had reached its logical conclusion: "disembodied leadership groups appealing to a mass membership."

The irony is that in order to pursue the public purpose of the farmer's freedom from the debt-peonage system, the new Populist Party had to look and act just like one of Hamilton's special interest political groups.

The leaders of the Populist Party appealed to farmers for support, as if the farmers were just like any other special interest group.

It is one of the lessons of history about political reform of Madison's system.

reform within his system is only possible if the political reform is organized and operates just like a special interest group.

In other words, the public interest must be seen as a private special interest, or as Madison described it, "a faction.".

In their brief political life as elected leaders in North Carolina, the Populists were successful in implementing many elements of banking reform that they had previously sought through the Democratic Party.

In The Promise of the New South, Edward Ayers wrote that they "established an impressive record."

They rewrote the anti-democratic election laws implemented by the Democrats, set limits on interest rates, restored local elected representation at the county level, put state money into every level of local schools, spent state taxes on charitable institutions and prisons, and finally, authorized the issuance of a historical text book for public schools entitled "School History of the Negro Race in the United States." (Ayers, Edward L., The Promise of the New South: Life After

Reconstruction, Oxford University Press, 1992.).

This last reform may have contributed more to the success of the political counter-attack against the Populists in the late 1890's by the Democrats than the rift in leadership described by Schwartz.

The counter-attack which was based upon the appeal of racism was bloody, violent, and lawless, and a complete success in killing the Populist Party.

The Democrat Party's goals in killing the Populist Party was described in the October 14, 1898, Goldsboro Daily Argus,

"In all that involves power, authority or privilege, concerning the affairs of the people and the relations of the races, the white people will rule this State."

Three weeks later, on November 10, 1898, the leaders of the North Carolina Democratic Party staged a military coup d'etat in Wilmington, deposing the city's elected leaders, and almost assassinated Governor Russell, the Republican Populist governor, who had come to Wilmington to calm the riot.

The white Democrats, however, made good on their promise for white Democrats to rule the state, which they did unchallenged for the next 100 years.

In the case of the Populists, the set of values of their reform effort was built around their critique of Madison's special interest political system.

Yet, the reforms themselves were well within the free market ideology of the Whigs.

In The Roots of Southern Populism, Steven Hahn summarizes the five major themes of the agrarians. (Hahn, Steven, The Roots of Southern Populism: Yeomen Farmers and the Transformation of the Georgia Upcountry, 1850-1890, Oxford University Press, 1983.).

First, the agrarians understood that the increasing wealth and economic power in the market place was transferring a certain range of unelected political privileges from economic affairs to political affairs.

That transfer of economic power translated into a political ability to exercise sovereign political power over farmers that was not in any way derived from the consent of the governed, and was not subject to reform through the mechanism of electoral politics.

The political power of special interests drew its sustenance from economic power, and was concentrated in the branches of the federal government, making local and state governments less able to ameliorate the effects of the elite's centralized power and privileges.

Second, the agrarians could see how the combination of economic power and privileges created the conditions of economic dependency for farmers.

Not only was capital and investment in the hands of the elites, thanks to Hamilton's banking system, but the police power of the state was being used to force farmers, against their will, to remain under the tutelage of the elite, through the operation of the debt-peonage contracts and tight money policies.

Farmers could never get out of debt, and were losing title to their lands, and had no path of escape and no path of upward occupational mobility.

They were slaves in a new type of slavery system, or to paraphrase C. B. MacPherson, farmers had become an economic "thing," whose interests did not really matter to the special interest elites in the nation's capital.

The only political interest that mattered in Washington was the ruling-class view of the national interest, which coincidentally, was exclusively the financial interests of the elite.

Third, the agrarians learned a tough political lesson that the machinery of the election system was totally corrupt.

It was corrupt in counting votes, corrupt in casting ballots, corrupt in conducting elections, corrupt in voter registration, and corrupt in distributing the "spoils" of the elections.

The voting process in the South was so corrupt that after the death of the Populist Party, most of the formerly elected Populist representatives at the local level were replaced by insider political appointments handled by the ruling Democratic Party officials in each state capital.

The corruption at the local and state level was compounded by corruption in election machinery at the federal government level.

Speaking in 1858, Georgia governor Joseph Brown said,

"It is already claimed by some that the banks now have the power by combinations and free use of large sums of money to control the political conventions and elections in our State, and in this way to crush those who may have the independence to stand by the rights of the people in opposition to their aggressive power."

Speaking on behalf of the Democrat Party elites, John Dent, a former plantation owner, argued in 1870, that the capitalists would be at the mercy of the common class unless their ability to vote was taken away.

Speaking of a recent election where the common citizens had voted against the interests of the capitalists, Dent said,

"Such voting show that capitalists and tax payers of the country are at the mercy of a class of men whose only capital are their votes...nothing but a restriction on the voters qualifications will ever protect capital from such injustice and wrongs..."

Fourth, the farmer's populist critique of Madison's political system contained a moral element about the worth and value of the individual.

The existing value system in place at the time emphasized a person's moral worth in terms of financial wealth, and this moral worth, following Locke, translated into political decision making power.

As Bill Cecil-Fronsman pointed out, the constitution,

"...reminded common whites that they were members of a society whose leaders regarded wealth as a legitimate measure of a man's worth." (Cecil-Fronsman, Bill, Common Whites: Class and Culture In Antebellum, University Press of Kentucky, 1992.).

The agrarians, in contrast, believed that a person's worth was derived from a loving God, who loved all individuals equally.

Finally, the agrarians had learned first hand the intricate relationship between the control of banking and money supply system and the legal system.

They understood how credit relationships between lenders and debtors could easily be extended into debt-peonage relationships wherein debtors lost their land and ended up in prison.

The farmers could also see first hand the effect of how a change in the Homestead Laws allowed bankers and merchants to extort land titles, under the guise of the rule of law.

The Populist leaders understood how the rule of law could be subverted, as eloquently expressed by Leonidas Polk, who said,

"To say that the unjust and ruinous exactions of capital and corporate power are made in conformity to law is no answer, for there is no tyranny so degrading as legalized tyranny, there is no injustice so oppressive as that which stands entrenched behind the forms of law."

When these five values of agrarian reform finally coalesced around the banner of the Populist Party, the spirit of individual freedom served to provide ideological coherency to the Populist criticisms of the American political system, and helped to guide Populists in making policy decisions.

As noted by V. O. Key, in Southern Politics In State and Nation,

"Philosophers and historians find the origin, if not the explanation, of this [American Democratic] spirit in the political struggles at the end of the past century, which propelled the state (of North Carolina) into its modern era of liberalized Democratic government." (Key, V. O. (Vladimer Orlando),with the assistance of Alexander Heard, Southern Politics in State and Nation, A. A. Knopf, 1949.).

The ideology of individual freedom embraced by the populists had its historical origins in the reforms to the constitution advocated by the anti-federalists, just called the "antis," in 1787.

According to Robert Goldwin,

"The Anti-Federalist's great concern was that the powers of the national government threatened the annihilation of the state governments...What was a danger to all liberty was an all-powerful central government able to tax from a great distance and thus render state and local government relatively powerless." (Goldwin, Robert A., From Parchment to

Power: How James Madison Used the Bill of Rights to Save the Constitution, AEI Press, 1997.).

While this value of local government over federal government started out its political life in the Anti-Federalist, Jefferson-Republican camp, its trajectory eventually took it to a new home in the Southern-Bourbon Democrat party.

As Lincoln noted, this political transformation was like two wrestlers who ended up in each other's coat.

Michael Perman, in The Road To Redemption, summarized the Bourbon principles as an emphasis on local government, decentralization of power within the federal system, noninterference by government in matters of individual behavior and belief, and laissez-faire economic policies. (Perman, Michael, The Road to Redemption: Southern Politics, 1869-1879, University of North Carolina Press, 1984.).

The emphasis on local government as a political value currently flies under the political banner of "state's rights."

In its usage under the Bourbon Democrat's "states rights," was used effectively, both before and after the Civil War, as a tool to bind common whites to the Democrat political party.

In an irony of history, what was once used by the Southern Democrats to bind common whites to the National Democrat Party, after the agrarian revolt, eventually became an effective tool for binding black voters to the National Democratic Party, since "state's rights," as a concept, became synonymous with the racism of Southern Democrats, who had initially used the term in its racist application to gain one-party control.

During the period of time leading up to the creation of the Populist Party, the Bourbon Democrats deployed the localist value to limit taxation on themselves, and, initially, to avoid using state government as a vehicle for internal improvements in roads and railroads.

Eventually, the Bourbons turned this opposition to internal improvements upside down, and used the concept of state's rights to defend state spending on internal improvements that benefited the financial interests of the bankers, merchants and industrialists who controlled the Southern Democratic Party.

The strange trajectory and use of the value of local government from the time of the Anti-Federalists is an example of what Lawrence Goodwyn described as the opportunistic use of cultural values for short term political gain by the two dominant parties.

Goodwyn wrote,

"Sectional, religious, and racial loyalties and prejudices were used to organize the nation's two major parties that ignored the economic interests of millions...Thus, the many-faceted Republican coalition that came to power in 1861 became in the postwar years a much narrower business party, closely tied to the politics of sectional division...the fact was central: sectional prejudices in the 1880's and 1890's persisted as an enormous political barrier to anyone bent on creating multi-sectional party of reform." (Goodwyn, Lawrence. Democratic Promise: The Populist Moment in America, Oxford University Press, 1976.).

By the time the value of local government reached the formation of the Populist

Party, it had already had a long and colorful career under the banner of the other two parties.

Under the domain of the Populists, the value of local government was attached to their realization that the growth in the power of central government had been accomplished, as Bruce Palmer noted,

"...in the hands of the plutocrats and wealthy who used that power to oppress the producers." (Palmer, Bruce, Man Over Money: The Southern Populist Critique of American Capitalism, University of North Carolina Press, 1980.).

This animosity of the farmers to central government in the hands of the elite was joined to Jefferson's Republican ideology that local self-government was an activity rooted in a particular place, carried out by citizens loyal to that place.

From the vantage point of many historians, this Southern Republican Populist stance towards local self-government has often been interpreted in an explanation of the common white citizen's ideological defense of slavery.

But, the Populist value of local government had much less to do with slavery, which was the predominate concern of the elite plantation class of Bourbon Democrats, than the broader cultural values of individuals defending local affairs against the intrusions on freedom by the elite, whether they were the intrusions of southern slave holders or of the financial plutocrats in Washington.

Eugene Genovese makes the point that the value of local government of the Populists coexisted with the Bourbon defense of slavery.

"So long as the slaveholders made few demands on these upcountry (white republican) regions, their claims to being champions of local freedom and autonomy against meddling outsiders appeared perfectly legitimate to the farmers." (Genovese, Eugene D., The Slaveholders' Dilemma: Freedom and Progress in Southern Conservative Thought, 1820-1860, University of South Carolina Press, 1992.).

In the hands of the slaveholder Bourbon Democrats, the value of local government was used as a ruse for political purposes to gain and maintain elected positions.

In the hands of Populists, the value was used as a guiding principle of how government should be organized to best promote individual freedom.

The second enduring cultural and social value of the Populists concerned the matrix of values surrounding their concept of individual equality and equal rights.

The philosophical basis for this matrix of values relates to the view the Populists had of relationships between people.

According to Palmer, in Man Over Money,

"The essential social relationship was between individuals, not between people and organizations...they considered the social order at bottom a network of personal relationships between human beings rather than impersonal relations between people and social organizations, such as the government, labor unions, courts, and corporations."

The lineage of this value of individualism in its political application is as complicated as the value on local government.

In the South, this notion that relationships were between individuals extended to the Southern conception of the constitution as a contract between individuals to defend each other's freedoms.

The common whites in the South, according to Cecil-Fronsman,

"...boldly asserted their independence and self-worth; they insisted that they were as good as anyone else. On the other hand, they lived in a society that made it plain that they were not."

Living in this social contradiction in the South led to many unusual arrangements and relationships between both common whites and plantation elites, and more interestingly, between common whites and free blacks.

Eventually, it was the threat posed by the political coalition of common whites and blacks, in the guise of the Republican Populist Party, which led to the violent 1898 counter-attack of the Bourbon Democrats, using the war cry of "Negro Rule" as their rallying point.

The value of individual equality in the South was linked to the concept of economic independence and self-sufficiency.

The definition of equality was derived from a condition of independence upon others, and freedom was achieved by acquiring sufficient land and resources to insure personal independence.

Common whites valued economic independency from the plantation elite, and despised the notion of dependency, which they equated with "laziness."

Allen Tullos commented upon this value in Habits of Industry: White Culture and the Transformation of the Carolina Piedmont, when he noted that,

"Farmer logic was powered by a commitment to personal independence, family self sufficiency, and neighborly interdependence...In the pursuit and maintenance of independence, the farm household itself became the yeomanry's most productive resource." (Tullos, Allen, Habits of Industry: White Culture and the Transformation of the Carolina Piedmont, University of North Carolina Press, 1989.).

As applied to politics, the telos, or end goal of common whites in the South, before and after the Civil War, was, according to Steven Hahn,

"...a commonwealth of independent producers for whom political liberty and personal freedom were inseparable from the patterns of mutuality in their settlements." (Hahn, Steven, The Roots of Southern Populism: Yeomen Farmers and the Transformation of the Georgia Upcountry, 1850-1890, Oxford University Press, 1983.).

It was Hahn's interpretation that in the Civil War, the common whites,

"fought for a liberty and independence not beholden to slaveownership, but rooted in communities of petty producers."

This value of individual equality in the South began long before the Civil War.

Traveling through the South at the turn of the eighteenth century, Charles Janson wrote that the common whites he met were,

"...extremely tenacious of the rights and liberties of republicanism. They consider themselves on an equal footing with the best people of the country and upon the principles of equality they intrude themselves into every company."

The origin of this value of individual equality lay in the southern yeoman tradition of subsistence farming.

Paul Escott notes in Many Excellent People, that,

"North Carolina's yeomen were, in reality, a self-directed, stubborn and independent group. Theirs was a traditional way of life based upon subsistence farming. It was neither luxurious not easy, but it offered self-reliance and self-respect." (Escott, Paul D., Many Excellent People: Power and Privilege in North Carolina, 1850¬1900, University of North Carolina Press, 1985.).

It is from the value of self-respect and independence that the farmers could grant a measure of respect and equality to others.

Escott goes on to write, that from the eyes of the plantation elite, the yeomen were not respectable, and tended to view them as unreliable and in the same class as free blacks and slaves.

This elite class conception of common whites endured for much of the 19th century.

Edward Ayers quotes Worth Bagley, a member of the plantation elite in 1892, that the Populists were,

"...perfect upstarts who desire to bring themselves up to a level with the best, imagining (political) office will do it. I hate the whole measly lot of pudding-headed demagogues."

Just as the value of local government could be made to serve the political needs of the Bourbon Democrats, this value of equality could be turned in such a way as to serve the needs of the elite.

After the Civil War, one of the ploys of the plantation elite was to play upon the element of individual honor of the Southern soldier by exhorting the soldiers to "vote as they shot," and to honor the traditions of the "Party of Their Fathers," which invoked the spirit of republicanism of Jefferson.

Jefferson, on the other hand, had written that,

"dependence begets subservience and venality, suffocates the germ of virtue, and prepares fit tools for the design of ambition...For this disease which destroys society and makes impossible the democracy of equality and independence, there is no remedy."

Jefferson admired the independent character of farmers which he believed corresponded to their economic independence, which was linked to their political independence.

In later years, the Agrarians invoked Jeffersons's "Spirit of `76," to describe their love of individual liberty and the right of republican self-government.

As long as the plantation elite could co-opt the Spirit of '76 with the claim that the ruling class represented the ideology of Jefferson, the political usurpation of those values would serve to bind farmers to the Democratic Party.

At the same time in history that the plantation elite was working to undermine the Populist Party's appeal to the farmer's values of independence, leaders of the "New South" plantation elite began a publicity campaign using the values of independence and republican self-government as a political ruse to obtain elected authority.

According to Michael Perman in The Road to Redemption, the New South leaders advocated the need for farmers to be independent and self sufficient, values the farmers deeply believed.

"To be prosperous, therefore, farmers must be, first, self-reliant, and, second, no longer at the mercy of external forces for their essential services and supplies...Self-reliance and independence for the individual farmer was the hallmark of the agricultural New South."

Because of their political appeal to the farmers, these values, in the hands of the Bourbon Democrats, led farmers deeper into the debt-peonage system.

Freedom and independence, for the elite, meant using the government for economic policies that predominantly benefited the elite.

In order for the elite to be free, large numbers of white and black farmers had to be denied freedom.

In order to deny farmers freedom, the farmer's had to believe that the Democrats were actually their political allies.

The "Party of Our Fathers" combined with the New South appeal of farmer "self-reliance" proved to be an irresistible political combination for attracting the farmers to the Democratic Party, a condition, as W. J. Cash noted in The Mind of the South, has never changed to this day. (Cash, W. J. (Wilbur Joseph), The Mind of the South: 1900-1941, 1st ed., Alfred A. Knopf, 1941.).

In the hands of the Populists, the value of individual equality served to undergird a system of equal political rights.

The values of individual freedom came first, and then, based upon a farmer's notion of his own rights, he extended those same rights to others.

As Zuckert noted in his writings about Jefferson,

"We come to respect those rights in others which we value in ourselves. Rights in the proper sense arise when human beings come to recognize a need for reciprocity in rights...that to claim a right for oneself requires accepting the same right in others...claims of rights become rights with duties reciprocal to them." (Zuckert, Michael P., The Natural Rights Republic:

Studies in the Foundation of the American Political Tradition, Rev. ed., University of Notre Dame Press, 1996.).

In the Populist ideology, the constitution is the contract which spells out the equal rights and duties of each citizen to defend the freedoms of others.

When it finally reached its new home in the Populist Party, and as the masthead of Tom Watson's paper, "equal rights for all" had traveled under the banner of many different political parties.

As Martin Wolfe observed,

"We've become like a nation of advertising men, all hiding behind catch phrases like "prosperity," "rugged individualism," and the "American Way." And, the real things that belonged to the American dream since the beginning – they have become just words too." (Wolf, Martin, Why Globalization Works, Yale University Press, 2004.).

The two dominant political values of local government and equal individual rights were linked to the third major enduring value embraced by the Populists that involved upward occupational mobility and economic opportunity.

Lawrence Goodwyn described Populism

"as a movement of ordinary Americans trying to gain control over their lives and futures." (Goodwyn, Lawrence. Democratic Promise: The Populist Moment in America, Oxford University Press, 1976.).

The control over their destiny was being denied by an unfair political and economic system which the Populists desired to reform.

"At issue," according to Bruce Palmer in Man Over Money,

"was not private ownership of wealth and property but their concentration in a few hands. A wider distribution of private property through equalization of opportunities would correct this."

The same interpretation of the Populist value is given by Carl Degler, in The Other South, who wrote,

"The Populists did not object to the system; they merely wanted a fair chance to prosper under it. They had been led to believe...that America was the home of opportunity." (Degler, Carl N., The Other South: Southern Dissenters in the

Nineteenth Century, 1st ed., Harper & Row, 1974.).

Writing in Progressive Farmer, the magazine that he founded, Leonidas Polk wrote,

"We do not wish to be rich but only want a reasonable chance that we may be able to achieve decent and respectable lives and educate our children. Surely no enemy could say anything against such a doctrine as this."

But, the Populists soon learned another important lesson of history.

Their political enemies had much to say against this value of upward mobility, and their enemies finally found a way to use the farmer's value of economic opportunity to their own advantage against the farmers.

Sadly, for the populists, Madison's rules, once established, provided no mechanism for the farmers to fight back, through the avenue of political reforms.

The initial reforms sought by the Populists aimed at the abuses primarily oriented to the agricultural economic issues of farmers.

Both the cooperative buying and selling programs, and Charles Macune's Sub-Treasury Plan sought reform that would correct the existing abuse of farmers in their role as neo-slaves in the debt-lien system.

At about the same time in history that these agricultural reforms were being proposed, a parallel economic vision began to be discussed that involved industrial mills, primarily those associated with cotton textiles.

It is a fiction of contemporary history that the impetus for the cotton textile mills originated with Northern industrial and financial interests in cooperation with New South visionaries.

The mills were seen by many in the farmer's movement as holding out hope that farmers and farm families could escape debt-peonage by becoming wage-earning manufacturing workers, in their home communities.

With money wages, the farmers reasoned, the farmers perhaps could achieve decent respectable lives and educate their children.

Beginning around 1873, the North Carolina agricultural granges of Mecklinburg, Cabarrus, and surrounding counties, began discussing how they could raise the initial capital to invest in a community-based textile mill.

According to Phillip Wood, in Southern Capitalism, these early discussions led to a type of community venture capital mutual fund, wherein farmers pooled their savings for the investment.

"By 1878, wrote Wood, "they had accumulated ninety thousand dollars, which they planned to use to build a mill in Gaston County." (Wood, Phillip J., Southern Capitalism: The Political Economy of North Carolina, 1880¬1980, Durham, N.C., Duke University Press, 1986.

The local pooling of capital for local industrial investment soon became a matter of great fervor for the farmers.

In 1873, the Greensboro paper urged the Patrons of Husbandry, also known as the Grange, to provide the organizational base upon which to encourage, create and solidify local industries.

"The aim of such an approach," wrote the editor, "was to confer the badge of civic virtue on mill building."

This local civic virtue was described by W. J. Cash, in The Mind of the South,

"The impulse leaps from community to community, as an electric current leaps across a series of galvanic poles – sweeping the citizens into mass assembly...it actually sets yeoman farmers, to poor as individuals to provide even so much as a single share of capital, to combining in groups of a dozen for the purpose; it sets laborers to forming pools into which each man pays as little as twenty-five cents a week."

A historical description of this phenomena of local farmers raising local investment capital is contained in Glen Gilman's piece, "The Folk Build the Mills," where he wrote,

"A relationship grew up between the communities and their mills that was, and has remained unique in an industrial region. The community built the mills, and the mills saved the communities. The mills "belong" to the communities."

This local allegiance to home community is entirely compatible with the cultural values the farmers had of local government and individual economic freedom.

Those two values were conjoined with the values of upward occupational mobility and the chance to achieve a decent life in the American dream mentioned by Martin Wolfe as individual freedom, equal opportunity, and the integrity and worth of the individual.

As the local mill building campaign gained momentum, the leader of the Populist Party cautioned that there needed to be diversification in the industrial base.

Leonidas Polk advocated, according to Stuart Noblin in his book on Polk, many small, diversified, industries for the South.

Polk said,

"It may be that we will yet learn that diversified industries is the surest foundation of prosperity, and that to increase these we must have less politics and give a little more time to business, talk less abut Southern independence, and work harder to bring it about."

At the same time in history that the early farmer groups were promoting both agricultural reforms and locally-owned industrial development, the plantation elite were preoccupied with re-asserting their own pre-war political value system.

The Bourbon Democrats had experienced the rigors of political competition with the post-war reconstruction Republicans and found the experience of sharing power with the Republicans distasteful.

According to Cash,

"The burning concern thus generated in the minds of the master class met with and married with that other concern which, as we have seen, was generated in them by their own economic difficulties...brought to a full conviction...that without ever abandoning cotton growing, the arm of the land must somehow be extended."

The solution for the master class, according to Cash, was pretty simple. For them, the economic future of the South should look just like its past.

Cash wrote,

"Progress was being accomplished so completely within the framework of the past that the plantation remained the single great basic social and economic pattern of the South...that is exactly what the Southern factory almost invariably was: a plantation."

This time, though, the labor force on the mill plantation would be provided by common whites, not by slave blacks.

Blacks had to be used by the elite to perform a different economic and political function than working in the mills.

In order to achieve their desired goal, the master class needed to manipulate the value of economic opportunity to serve their needs.

The pathway of attack was along the farmer's intersection of values of individualism and local allegiance to community and family.

Bruce Palmer described how the Bourbon Democrats began

"...an effort to reconcile individual material self interest with the welfare of the community, (which) led to the abandonment of the core of the (farmer's) former idea – that society was held together and progressed because of the action of each person's material self-interest – and moved toward a consideration of society as a group of people (white) rather than a collection of individuals."

This was the beginning of the modern version of group welfare collectivism that so effectively holds the Democratic Party together today.

Within each town and community where the mill building fervor of the farmers arose, the merchants and landowners, who were already attached to the Bourbon Democrats, began assuming control over the industrial building enterprises.

They formed local boosterism clubs to promote their communities as a desirable location for a mill.

The ruling class financial interest in this boosterism was easy to understand, according to Gavin Wright.

"Virtually every industrial beginning may be traced to someone's attempt to make a capital gain on property in land by selling the land for the industrial plant. (Wright, Gavin, Old South, New South: Revolutions in the Southern Economy Since the Civil War, Basic Books, 1986.)

By virtue of their debt-peonage system of taking the land from the farmers, the elite now were land-rich and needed the government to help them convert their land to cash.

Paul Escott quotes a farmer, J. A. Wilson, from Mecklinburg County, N. C., speaking in 1894,

"Owing to legislation in favor of monopolies, our lands are gradually slipping away from the hands of the wealth-producing classes and going into the hands of the few."

Industrial recruitment allowed the elite to use the agencies of government to bring buyers to their land, with the government providing cash to the elite in the industrial recruitment strategy.

The historical continuity of this ploy is remarkable for its endurance to this day and time.

The Democrats throughout the South began passing a series of laws, known as "anti-enticement laws" that made it illegal to entice a farmer from the land of his Landlord, or to "aid or abet" the farmer in transportation from the land.

In conjunction with the Landlord-Tenant Acts, which made it a felony to remove crops from the land without the Landlord's approval, the system of laws in the South were effective at eliminating opportunities for economic advancement.

As noted by Wood, the combination of laws,

"allowed the planters to create a labor force whose freedom was severely curtailed by the indebtedness arising from the operation of the lien system and reinforced by the actions of the State."

The urge to make a quick buck on land deals though does not explain how the Bourbon Democrats assumed control of the mill building enterprise by turning one of the farmer's core values against them.

In the industrial recruitment boosterism rhetoric, the merchants and land owners promoted the town's economic wealth as a collective enterprise.

Following Wright,

"there was a sense in which the beneficiaries really could be seen as 'the community' ...What was most misleading about the cotton mill rhetoric was the implication that non-property owning (white) laborers and concern for their welfare played a major role" in the booster's motivations."

The master class was using the appeal of "more and better jobs" for the 'community' in a way that appealed to the farmer's need for upward mobility while at the same time, undermining the farmer's traditional values of individual freedom.

The farmer's cherished value of individual freedom gave way to a new form of economic dependency that re-established the plantation hierarchy in the form of a mill paternalism.

"The essence of the mill paternalism," according to I. A. Newby, in Plain Folk in the New South,

"derived not from the exploitation it facilitated but the reciprocal relationship it defined...the mill folk explained and rationalized their dependency (in a way) that enabled them to acknowledge and act on it without losing their sense of individuality and self-worth." (Newby, I. A. (Idus A.), Plain Folk in the New South: Social Change and Cultural Persistence,

1880-1915, Louisiana State University Press, 1989.).

In other words, under the new social contract of mill paternalism, the farmer's were persuaded to give up on their values of economic freedom in exchange for the promise of "more and better jobs" that would be delivered by the Bourbon Democrats, who assumed control over the process of industrial recruitment.

From a moral values point of view, the organizational image of society was converted by the Bourbons from one that featured relationships between individuals to one that stressed the communal values of the local town, a concept very close to the hearts of the farmers.

According to Cash,

"The southern textile industry stressed communal values. Its image for social relationships in mill villages was not the market but the paternalistic family."

Under the jurisdiction of the plantation elite, the mill building movement used the values of the Populists, individual initiative, ambition and economic independence, which led to social

140

relationships in mill towns that featured, according to Newby,

"a kind of social atomism, suspicion of strange people and new ideas, and resistance to social innovation of any sort," including the political innovations promoted by the Populists."

McMath points out that the plantation elite were successful at perpetuating a myth of progress associated with the mill villages that eventually turned into a myth about the virtues of industrial recruitment schemes.

The myths

"...implied that commercial and industrial endeavors centered in the region's towns and cities would rejuvenate the southern economy and that the forging of a politically solid (white) South, presided over by the lords of factory, firm and plantation, would restore a Golden Age of southern politics." (McMath, Robert C., Populist Vanguard: A History of the Southern Farmers' Alliance, Norton, 1975.).

There is a big difference in the historical interpretation what the "Golden Age" in America after the Civil War meant.

In the minds of the master class, the Golden Age meant the restoration of their unelected, unchallenged position of political authority.

This interpretation of southern history has become conventional wisdom because it plays so neatly into a monolithic liberal explanation needed by the Democratic Party elites that everything about the South revolves around the issue of slavery and racism.

In contrast to what the master class desired, in the minds of the farmers and the Populists, the Golden Age meant trying to restore some semblance the values of Jefferson republicanism, that features a society of equal rights for all and special privileges for none.

The myth of community progress perpetuated by the master class was effective in drawing the support of the mill workers away from the Populist movement and lodging it firmly in the camp of the Bourbon Democrats.

The myth was purchased at a high cost for the common white farmers, and at an appallingly high cost to Southern Blacks.

According to Cash,

"...the cotton mill worker of the South would be stripped of his ancient autonomy and placed in every department of his life under the control of his employer."

At about the same time in history that the Bourbon Democrats were assuming political control over the industrial mill-building schemes, changes in textile mill production techniques were occurring that allowed less-skilled workers to be matched on the production floor with automated equipment.

This coincidence of events, the ruling class political control, coupled with the economic control, opened up a new opportunity for the Bourbon Democrats to merge the myth of progress associated with mill building with aggressive industrial recruitment of northern textile corporations, using the lure of low wages, tax benefits and credits as recruitment incentives.

Phillip Wood, in Southern Capitalism, cites the case in 1895, of a southern industrial recruiter making a pitch to northern textile manufacturers to move south.

In his appeal to the New England Cotton Manufacturing Association, Edmonds told the manufacturers that they could not overcome the major southern advantage,

"...a large, and at that point, mostly untapped supply of poor white workers, who were docile, not given to strikes, and as a class, were anxious to find work and willing to accept much lower wages than northern operatives."

The appeal to northern interests to move south, based upon the "docility of the workers," and their eagerness to accept lower wages, is the defining characteristic of how the Bourbon Democrats turned the values of the farmers for upward occupational mobility against them.

The common whites were docile because they believed in economic development that would benefit their local towns and communities.

They were eager to accept low wages because they desperately wanted to achieve upward occupational mobility, and were willing to start on the lower rungs on the ladder of opportunity.

The economic outcome for the farmers was economic growth in the number of jobs, without wide distribution of economic prosperity.

The system implemented by the Bourbon Democrats had no mechanism to reinvest profits derived from the northern textile mills back into the home communities.

To the extent that southern mill owners made profits from the industrial recruitment schemes, these profits were generally not re-invested in the towns and villages that would have perpetuated a cycle of self-sustaining, self-renewing economic development.

The profits went, in many cases into building huge mansions and lovely private universities.

According to Cash,

"...by 1910, the barons and the stockholders of the mills were exhibiting a tendency to turn a smaller proportion of the total profits back to building of more mills or the expansion of industry and business in general, and to take more for their own personal purposes."

As long as the capital investment gap created by industrial recruitment could be filled by recruiting more outside investment, the Bourbon Democrats would achieve their ultimate goal: the re-establishment of the plantation, and their unchallenged legal right to exercise monopoly political authority.

Once in place, the mill workers/farmers had no constitutional pathway of reform of the neo-plantation mill system.

According to Paul Escott, the

"Elite Democrats did more than beat back the challenge of the Populists, disfranchise black people, and stigmatize cooperation between Tar Heels of both races. They imposed an undemocratic electoral system, so complete and effective that all future political discourse had a restricted character."

After 100 years of their economic policy and one-party rule, what remains in place according to Jack Bass and Walter DeVries, is a

"...political plutocracy that lives with a progressive myth." (Bass, Jack, and DeVries, Walter, The Transformation of Southern Politics: Social Change and Political Consequence Since 1945, University of Georgia Press, 1995.).

The historical legacy of the myth is that it turned the cultural values of the farmers against them, and once entrenched in the political fabric, it served to continually undermine the Populists values of "equal rights for all and special privileges for none."

The lessons of history drawn from the Populist experience of attempting political reform in America can be categorized into three topic headings.

First the Populist experience offers lessons in politics for the creation of third party movements in America that aim to compete with the Democrats and Republicans on the issue of more citizen control over the political process.

Second, the Populist efforts at economic cooperative programs and reform of the banking system teach lessons about both the workings of the free enterprise system in the context of Madison's special interest political system and the cultural values of freedom that are associated with competitive free markets.

Finally, the Populist emphasis on the cultural values of equal rights and individual freedom offers philosophical lessons about what holds societies together in joint cooperative constitutional democracies.

As noted by McMath, in Populist Vanguard,

"Without the promise of direct, individual benefit through the cooperatives, most Alliance farmers would not, except for a relatively brief time, commit themselves to working for generalized political objectives."

Schwartz makes the same point in Radical Protest and Social Structure, where he writes,

"The understanding that mutual benefits can be gained only by first making mutual sacrifices is the keystone of the organization. But, this understanding is activated only when the individual firmly believes that the action will succeed."

The populists learned that hard work, and playing by Madison's rules, does not insure financial success or lead to upward occupational mobility in America.

They had the right set of moral values about work, and allegiance to play by the rules, but labored under Madison's unfair rules.

Leonidas Polk, who founded N. C. State University, said,

"Labor is thus associated in our mind with all that is honorable in birth, refined in manners, bright in intellect, manly in character and magnanimous in soul."

For the populists, hard work was associated with the value of independence and the moral value of a person.

In the Savage Ideal, Bruce Clayton notes that in the South,

"work was a moral absolute, an outer sign of inner worth..." (Clayton, Bruce D., The Savage Ideal: Intolerance and Intellectual Leadership in the South, 1890-1914, Johns Hopkins University Press, 1972.).

The farmers learned a tough lesson about work after the Civil War, as the debt-peonage system tightened its grip.

The lesson was captured by Goodwyn, in his article, "The Cooperative Movement."

"At settlin' up time, the farmer and the merchant would meet at the cotton gin, where the fruits of year's toil would be ginned, bagged, tied, weighed, and sold. At that moment, the farmer would learn what his cotton had brought. The merchant, who had possessed title to the crop, even before the farmer had planted it, then consulted his ledger for a final time. The accumulated debt for the year, he informed the farmer, exceeded the income from the crop."

The farmer, in the vernacular of the time, had "failed to payout."

There was no escape, no way out of debt.

The debt-lien laws held the farmer on the land for the next year, in the new slavery system, and would keep him there, year after year.

As the crop-lien system collapsed, under the tight money policies that devastated the commodity agriculture system, the hard-working farmers were offered a new form of slavery, as low wage mill workers.

This new system was even more vicious than the crop-lien system in that it captured the whole family.

Rather than paying each worker a wage, the mill owners would pay a family wage, but not in cash.

The family wage was paid in script, only redeemable at the mill store, owned by the mill owner.

According to Phillip Wood, the family would have its wages withheld for a period of four weeks, during which time,

"they would have accumulated four weeks' debt for supplies at the company store at increased 'advance' prices."

Every member of the family, beginning at age 6, worked in the mill, usually for 16 hours per day, and like the debt-peonage system of the farm, the family never got out of debt and had no economic path of escape.

In Habits of Industry, Tullos describes the

"...historical process in which the industrial fathers held a strong upper hand over desperate families who came to the mills already accustomed to long days and years of punishing physical labor for little reward."

According to Tullos, the farmers, both on the farm and later in the mills, learned, that "by itself, hard work could establish little."

It was in these historical circumstances provided by the new mill slavery system in the South that prompted Tom Watson, in 1891, to ask in his newspaper, "What is Labor's fair share?" he answered by saying that labor should,

"get all it makes after due allowance for material and the use of capital."

The political advantages of the ruling class were embedded into Madison's constitutional rules.

Once the rules were embedded, the rules did not leave farmers with any means of escape.

The public purpose of citizen sovereignty in Madison's special interest political system does not contribute campaign cash or other resources to getting candidates from either party elected.

There is nothing in Madison's constitutional rules directing the political party to protect the public purpose of individual freedom or national sovereignty.

Both the Republicans and the Democrats are committed to the two party status quo arrangement of politics that features special interest manipulation of the government and manipulation of rules to benefit the special interests within each party.

As Micheal Zuckert described it in The Natural Rights Republic, to be an American means accepting the universal truths contained in the Declaration of Independence.

Those truths were held, by Jefferson, to be self-evident, meaning outside of a chain of logic, and not derived from any other propositions.

They are held to be,

"...self-evident within the political community dedicated to making them effective."

The Populists were right about the threat to citizen sovereignty posed by the huge business trusts in the Gilded Age, and the consolidated power of bankers and merchants.

Before them, the followers of Jackson were right to fear the unelected power of the National Bank.

Before them, Jefferson and George Mason were correct in their assessment that Madison's constitutional arrangement

153

would reward a very small set of special interests.

The common citizen fear of ruling class privilege exercised in a political special interest system provides a great historical continuity in America that serves to guide the creation of a new constitutional democratic republic.

The great virtue of the competitive free market system is that voluntary, cooperative social behavior coordination can be achieved without tyranny and totalitarianism.

According to Adam Smith, the free market system leads to a social institutional order where all classes of citizens benefit.

The implementation of that voluntary, cooperative system though, depends, as Jefferson observed, on a belief and faith that individuals are their own best guardians of individual welfare.

Madison, and the Federalists, feared the people, in their capacity as individual citizens.

Madison started out his constitution reform with the phrase "We the people," as if to suggest that the parties to the contract were the individual citizens in the individual states.

Madison's idea was to spread special interests across a wide geographical area, and hope that the interests would not form coalitions across territory.

Once Madison implemented his system, he insured that common citizens would never see their own class interests the same way that Madison's natural aristocracy saw their own social class interests.

At the time he wrote his rules, the natural aristocracy already had a coherent social class consciousness of their own financial interests, and also had a coherent view of the threat posed by common citizens, if the common citizens ever attained equal rights.

Madison insured that the common citizens would never form a middle class consciousness by dispersing the political interests of common citizens across the fruited plain, so that disperse geographical interests would never coalesce into social class awareness.

Madison's divided government framework, that functions on the basis of majority rule decision making in each branch, prevents the formation of a national consensus on what constitutes the "public purpose" of government.

The lessons of history that the Agrarians taught was that reform of Madison's existing system, by common citizens, is impossible.

The farmers in the 1880s were never going to be successful in reforming the debt-lien system because Madison insulated the financial and economic agencies of government from the reforms desired by common citizens.

The farmers were successful in creating a social class consciousness of their own class interests, similar to the ruling class consciousness, which existed in 1787.

Through their mass educational meetings throughout the South, the farmers overcame one of Madison's barriers to having common citizens form a social class consciousness.

The important lesson of history is that a mass social movement, with a social class consciousness, must have its own political vehicle to implement reforms.

Reform for the farmers was never going to be accomplished within the corrupt two-party system.

Even with their own political party, the farmers were never going to achieve a fair distribution of political rights under Madison's British social class conflict model because Madison truncated the distribution of political rights.

The better path to freedom for the farmers and for common citizens, today, is the one advocated by Brennon and Buchanan to adopt a new set of constitutional rules that places individual liberty as the mission of government in the Preamble.

Chapter 4. Madison's Permanent Barriers to Common Citizen Political Reform in America.

Thomas Jefferson noted that the world seemed to be divided into two philosophical camps regarding an individual's capacity for self-government.

He wrote that there was one set of philosophical believers who thought that individuals were the best guardians of their own welfare, and were capable of self-rule.

The other philosophical camp identified by Jefferson held a different belief about the individual's capacity for self-government.

The other conception emphasized that individuals were not capable of self-government, and that group collectivism and elite rule would provide the best outcomes of social welfare.

From his own set of beliefs about self-government, Jefferson was able to derive a number of fundamental principles about government, among them that the government that governs best is that which governs the least and closest to the people, and that all legitimate authority is derived from the consent of the governed.

For Jefferson, the consent of the governed is not simply and exclusively a single event, obtained in the initial contract, when the citizens agree to leave the state of nature.

Jefferson believed that citizens provide on-going consent to follow the rules, as long as everyone in society is also following the constitutional rules.

The constitutional rules would establish a priority of local and state governments over national governments based on the principle that those bound most tightly by collective rules must be given the greatest say in the making and enforcing of the rules.

This priority of local and state governments over national government has a very subtle point about equality before the law.

If all individuals are equal in the making and enforcing of the law, and the law is applied most stringently at the most local level of the community, then no individual is greater, or above, the law.

In order to promote the greatest level of individual freedom, all individuals must be bound, in equal capacity, by the same law that they have given to themselves.

The priority of local government is related to how local laws most directly affect the individual in his or her every day pursuit of sovereignty.

It is the local zoning law that commands a certain use of land, the local property tax that consumes income, and local occupational and business licensing laws that most immediately affect life's opportunities and choices.

Prior to entering into the initial constitutional contract, Jefferson claimed, in the Declaration, that there must be a set of certain minimum moral values, in the ambient culture, to allow some minimal level of shared values about morality and truth to be exchanged.

Jefferson's passionate advocacy of public education was not based upon the cramped intellectual argument that common citizens needed practical job skills to compete in the market place, or the traditional religious argument that education was essential for citizens to understand Christian doctrine.

Rather, Jefferson understood that public education provided an institution that would facilitate on-going civic education for common citizens.

Citizens would be continually educated about their civic responsibility, in a public education forum not dominated by the elite social class ideology that common citizens are incapable of self-government.

The instrumental value of public education for Jefferson in a democracy relates to the process of teaching citizens to respect the freedoms of other citizens, who view each other as political equals, under the law.

In Jefferson's concept of two competing social class ideologies about citizen self-rule, this form of public education would empower individual citizens with "structural power," to protect and defend their natural rights.

In Jefferson's second observation about self-rule, citizens are deemed irrational and must be kept in a state of "structural ignorance."

In the first constitutional contract of 1777, The Articles of Confederation identified individual liberty as the shared cultural value of the Revolution, and agreed with Jefferson that all citizens had the innate ability for self-government, when the citizens left the state of nature, after the Revolution ended.

In the second constitutional contract, of 1787, Madison identified social class competition between financial factions as the cultural value to guide his rules, based upon his philosophy that common citizens did not have an innate capacity for self-government.

Madison wrote the rules based upon his fear that American common citizens could possibly develop a class consciousness that would compete with the American natural aristocracy.

His false assumption about American common citizens was based upon his observation that the working classes in England already had developed a class consciousness.

As Hamilton explained during the Convention,

"Every community divides itself into hostile interests of the few and the many, the rich and well-born against the mass of people If either of these interests possessed all the power it would oppress the other...we (the well born) need to be rescued from the democracy."

Or, as James Dickinson, one of the 38 self-selected elite "Framers" stated at the convention in 1787, the new constitution must protect,

"the worthy against the licentious."

Dickinson explained that Madison's new Federal constitution placed the remedy of common citizen social disorder [Shays Rebellion] in the hands (well born) which feel the disorder of democracy, whereas the antifederalists placed the remedy in the hands of citizens (the common people), who cause the disorder, by not paying their taxes and debts in gold and silver.

Madison's goal was to prevent the "tyrannical concentration of all the powers of government in the same hands." [of a consolidated majority of common citizens].

Michael Klarman, in his book. The Framers Coup, (Oxford University Press, 2016.), described Madison's concept of society.

Klarman wrote,

"Madison viewed society as two classes: creditors or debtors, rich or poor... Madison declared that the Senate [wealthy faction] ought to come from and represent the wealth of the nation. The Senate should serve as a bastion of privilege. Dickinson wanted the Senate to bear the likeness of the British House of Lords. Pinckney argued that, "only the wealthy would be able to afford to serve."...As Butler put it, "the great object of government was to protect property...the Senate would block any populist economic measures that might emanate from the [elected common citizens] in the House."

Madison said that the unelected Senate needed to be a "check on the democracy. It cannot be made too strong."

As described by Wilentz, Madison's concept of society was that the natural aristocracy represented,

"a class of citizens who deserved to claim a disproportionate share in the direction of public affairs." (Wilentz, Sean, The Rise of American Democracy: Jefferson to Lincoln, W. W. Norton & Co., Inc., 2005.).

John Adams predicted the outcome of Madison's hypothetical social class conflict by noting that Madison's constitutional rules would permanently divide the nation into two groups, creditors and debtors.

According to Adams, the purpose of Madison's constitution was to

"...settle wealth and power upon a minority. It will be accomplished by a national debt, paper corporations, and offices, civil and military. These will condense king, lords and commons, a monied faction and an armed faction in one interest."

Madison's permanent barriers to political reform of constitutional rules by common citizens occurred at the very inception of his rules, based upon his philosophy that common citizens lacked the ability to participate in self-government.

His understanding of the inability of common citizens to engage in self-government was derived from his social class awareness that it had been the

American natural aristocracy's economic connection to the British aristocracy, during the colonial era, that benefitted the financial welfare of the American natural aristocracy.

Gouverneur Morris, a Federalist elite from New York, who strangely represented Pennsylvania at the Convention, instead of New York, stated in 1774, that the British connection was the guarantee of the existing aristocratic order…after the revolution, they engaged with Federalists in other states in undoing the Articles of Confederation.

As Madison admitted, in his 1792 essay, A Candid State of Parties,

"…some of the supporters of the Constitution openly or secretly are attached to monarchy and aristocracy."

He noted that the Federalists had,

"debauched themselves into a persuasion that mankind [common citizens] are incapable of governing themselves, and believed that government can only be carried on by the pageantry of rank, the influence of money and emoluments, and the terror of military force."

Strangely, four years earlier, at the Convention, Madison has been a part of this debauchment when he supported the resolution of John Dickinson, a federalist delegate from Delaware, on the creation of the Senate.

Dickinson's resolution on the creation of the Senate stated that,

"we ought to carry it through such a refining process as will assimilate it as near as may be to the House of Lords in England."

Ensuing generations of American common citizens did not realize that Madison had disconnected the cultural value of liberty, in The Articles of Confederation from Jefferson's Declaration, and connected his constitution to the British social class mixed government model, but without the British safeguards against ruling class tyranny provided by the intervention of the king.

Madison relied on the principles of separation of power from Edmund Burke, the British political philosopher who inspired Madison's constitutional work on creating a representative republic.

(Edmund Burke, Thoughts on the Present Discontents, 1770.).

Burke's ideas of a "mixed" government provided the philosophical justification for separation of government power in the American representative republic, which Madison adopted for his constitution.

The term "mixed" as used by Burke, refers to the "mix" of social classes who each share a portion of power in a "mixed" government.

Burke thought that by distributing and balancing government power between the King, the nobility and the commoners, that tyranny would be avoided.

He was careful to distinguish between legitimate criticisms of the King, when the King over-stepped his authority, and the more partisan parliamentary class politics between the elite, in the House of Lords, and the hurly-burly, in the House of Commons.

Without the King and his Council, the British system has no ultimate source of power or authority to distinguish between right and wrong.

Determining right from wrong is not the same thing as avoiding tyranny, and Burke was more concerned about avoiding tyranny than he was about obtaining justice.

Burke had written that an independent judiciary was absolutely necessary to provide stability and continuity in government.

For Madison, the separation of power would create a more perfect union that resembled the British mixed government, where the nobility were insulated from the common citizens.

Madison accepted Burke's primacy of avoiding tyranny, but in place of the King's role in determining right from wrong, Madison substituted an independent Federal judiciary, that was insulated from the democratic impulse.

Madison inserted the independence of the judiciary into the constitution, and aimed its function at preventing his definition of tyranny, not obtaining justice.

By creating a judiciary that was disconnected from the democratic consent of the governed, as the "Supreme" law of the land, Madison's truncated version of the British mixed system created a permanent barrier for common citizens to reform his constitution.

Unlike the citizens in England, where the King removes bad judges, the U. S. citizens have no way of removing the tyrannical Federal judges who serve for life.

Madison also accepted from Burke the definition that the primary source of tyranny would be the majority of common citizens oppressing the minority of the natural aristocracy.

Madison thought that the democratic majorities in each state legislature were oppressing the wealthy minority of bond holders and land speculators by allowing common citizens to pay their taxes in worthless paper money, and not in gold and silver.

In Madison's conception of mixed government, the constitution exists to provide rules for institutional sharing of power between social classes in their capacity of special interests, (the natural aristocracy and common citizens), and if rights inure to social groups, then, pro-social rule adherence depends on the separation of institutional power, not voluntary citizen allegiance to obey the rule of law.

The separation of power would work well, according to Madison, if there was unequal access by those without power to make claims against those who had institutional power (natural aristocracy).

Once Madison's constitutional contract had been established, he believed that institutional separation of power would perform the same political function as George Mason's proposed Bill of Rights.

Madison's version of the British mixed system also left out the part about the British multi-party parliamentary system.

Madison reasoned that, if there were only two social classes in America, that there would only be two political parties.

The two-party system in America creates a permanent barrier to common citizens reforming the government because they have no authority over the Supreme Court.

One political party, the Federalist natural aristocracy, had a coherent social class consciousness of its own financial interests.

Common citizens did not have a coherent social class consciousness, at the time of the Convention, and Madison's rules of the "extended republic," insured that the common citizens would never develop a coherent class consciousness to threaten the natural aristocracy.

Madison did not incorporate the British multi-party parliamentary system, but preferred to impose a static, two-class interpretation of society, leading to a static, unchanging two-party political system, that operates on the principle of ruling class shared plunder, not on representing the natural rights of common citizens.

In Madison's British Social Class mixed government, the goal of government is to ameliorate the class conflict between the natural aristocracy and common citizens.

Whenever Madison speaks of separation of powers, he is speaking from the social class perspective of what is in the best interests of the natural aristocracy, not from the perspective of the common good, or common wealth, of all citizens.

Justice means following Madison's civil rules of procedure in the courts, especially in civil cases involving disputes about property and paying taxes in gold and silver.

Madison's interpretation of Burke's definition of majority tyranny in conjunction with the independence of the Federal judiciary, created an unbalanced separation of power that eventually devolved into the old form of tyranny, where a tiny minority (9 Supreme Court justices), rule unchecked and beyond challenge, over a vast majority.

In Great Britain, the prime minister is accountable to the King, and Madison was not certain how the American President would function, in the absence of a King.

Madison's role model of President was Lord North, who was Prime Minister of Great Britain from January, 1770 to March, 1782.

When Madison wrote the Virginia Plan, in 1787, he replicated parts of the British model of Prime Minister, including the role of the King's Privy Council, redefined as the Virginia Council of State.

In the Virginia Plan model, the role of the prime minister in reporting to the King in Britain was replaced by Virginia's plantation elite, who were appointed to serve as the new Privy Council.

In other words, in Madison's Virginia Plan, the plantation elite were equivalent to the British nobility, who served on the King's Privy Council.

Madison created a version of the British King in his rules for the Presidency, and left the rules about the power of the President undefined, until the end of the Convention.

The Committee of Detail was given its task to define the powers of the President on July 24, 1787.

The job of the Committee of Detail was to add the final details to the resolution, before the adjournment of the Convention, tentatively set for September 13.

In its only major decision, the Committee of Detail decided that the title for the president should not be "king."

The other issues regarding the mission of the president and the rules for electing the president were left unsolved, to the very last minute.

The tasks of the Committee of Detail were eventually handed off to the Brearly Committee.

On September 4, 1787, the Brearly Committee reported an entirely new text and description of the Office of the Presidency, which did not conform to the debate about the Presidency in the prior 11 days.

The Brearly report replicated many of the executive powers of the British Prime Minister, but without the burden of the President reporting to the King, or to the King's Privy Council.

In other words, in Madison's version of the mixed government, the President does not report to anyone, which is one of the reasons why George Mason was so adamant about the absence of an Executive Council of State to advise the President.

Just prior to the end of the Convention, the delegates still had not agreed on the Brearly Committee powers of the Presidency.

The issue of the Presidency, was handed off to the Committee on Style, on September 8.

The Committee on Style, appointed 3 days before formal public debate at the Convention ended, on September 11, never released the final clauses of Article II, on the Presidency to the delegates, before they voted on them, on September 15.

In other words, the two most important rules of the Constitution, concerning slavery and the Presidency, were drafted in secret, and never presented to the delegates for debate, before they signed the document, on September 17, 1787.

The debate in the final 11 days of the Convention, before the Brearly report, revolved around what force acted as a barrier to a rogue President taking the law into his own hands.

Both proponents and opponents to the Constitution understood the danger of corruption and cabal of a rogue President, especially a rogue President who had formed a cabal with the aristocrats in the Senate.

The opponents to Madison's Virginia plan argued that the Office of President that Madison was creating was an unchecked power that would end in the tyranny of a rogue president.

Most of the authority for selecting the President was vested in the unelected Senate.

The Senate was comprised of a very tiny minority of America's natural aristocracy, and Madison's plan empowered the Senate make decisions about the election of the President.

Madison explained, in Federalist #47, how his rendition of the President, in the mixed government, would operate.

From Madison's Federalist.

"In the very Constitution to which it is prefixed, a partial mixture of powers has been admitted. The executive magistrate has a qualified negative on the legislative body, and the Senate, which is a part of the legislature, is a court of impeachment for members both of the executive and judiciary departments. The members of the judiciary department, again, are appointable by the executive department, and removable by the same authority on the address of the two legislative branches."

At the time Madison wrote his rules, he had in mind the political dissent of Shays'

Rebellion, which he considered to be common citizen tyranny because the farmers were not following the rules of paying taxes and debts in gold and silver.

Legitimate dissent, in Burke's conception, was based upon how the dissent was related to preventing tyranny.

Madison inserted his clause "to insure domestic tranquility" in the Preamble to provide the Federal Government with the power to quell any such further dissent by common citizens, which they did in 1794, when an army of 13,000 soldiers marched to Western Pennsylvania to quell the Whiskey Rebellion.

Like the farmers in Shays Rebellion, the farmers in Western Pennsylvania were not paying their taxes in gold and silver, which Hamilton needed to pay government bond holders full face value for the war bonds they had bought for pennies on the dollar.

Madison's beliefs about the benefits of his separation of power in the constitution were so strong that during the Convention, he adamantly opposed the adoption of the Bill of Rights.

He stated that the constitutional institutional arrangement that he created (a more perfect union), did not require the parchment barriers to tyranny.

In Madison's rule of law, the cultural value of shared individual liberty, in Jefferson's Declaration, was replaced with the British social class cultural value of shared plunder, in the "spoils system."

There is a sense of equality in Madison's constitutional rules because the elites all shared equally in the social value of plundering the system, without social class competition from common citizens.

During Virginia's ratifying convention, Patrick Henry wrote:

"Tell me not of checks on paper; but tell me of checks founded on self-love. The people's liberties are less safe under the proposed Constitution than under the British monarchy, for there [in England] at least the hereditary nobility have a stake in maintaining a balance between king and Commons; their continued existence depends on it. What corresponding incentives did the American analogues possess?"

During the same Virginia convention, James Monroe cited the differences between the authentic British mixed social class system and the truncated version that Madison created.

Monroe wrote,

"The English constitution is based upon social orders which have a repellent quality which enabled it to preserve itself from being destroyed by the other. The American division of power had no such basis and, indeed, no such intention. There are no real checks in the Constitution that would prevent a coalition of the branches of government and encroachments on the rights of the people."

Merrill Peterson, in The Jefferson Image in the American Mind, cited Madison's failure to establish Jefferson's concept of shared liberty as the mission, or purpose of government, in his Preamble.

Peterson wrote:

"that Madison's division of powers became the chief means of checking the exaggeration of the democratic principle, and thus of securing an equilibrium of majority power and constitutional guarantees…" (Peterson, Merrill D., The Jefferson Image in the American Mind, Oxford University Press, 1960.).

Madison's phrase, "We, the people," was a mythical, imaginary, collectivist idea that the 38 signers of the document were actually "We, the people."

We, the people only existed every four years, on election day.

As he did with the rules on the Presidency, and the Fugitive Slave Clause, Madison modified the text in the Preamble at the end of the Convention.

From Madison's notes: September 12, 3 days before the vote on the text.

"Committee of Style reported an amendment to Article 7, which was read by paragraph. This document (the Constitution), is preceded by a preamble, which begins, "We the People of the United States, in order to form a more perfect union…" rather than "We the people of the states of New Hampshire, etc…"

The other delegates had never seen this version of the Preamble before.

The text that they had seen before September 12, referenced the people of each state, which would have been consistent with King George's transfer of sovereignty to the 13 states.

"A more perfect union," said Thomas Paine, about Madison's flawed Preamble, "meant a nominal nothing without principles."

Patrick Henry stated,

"The US Constitution of 1787 is an ill-advised attempt to replicate the British form of mixed constitution. ..their basis for justice becomes the balancing of particular class interests....they make it difficult for [common] citizens to participate."

As Sean Wilentz wrote, in his book, The Rise of American Democracy: Jefferson to Lincoln,

"[We] The people had no formal voice of their own in government. And, that was exactly how it was supposed to be – for once the electors had chosen their representatives, they ceded power, reserving none for themselves until the next election...[We]The people, as a political entity, existed only on election day."

In his book, The Articles of Confederation, Merrill Jensen answers Centinel's question about how citizen sovereignty would work in Madison's rules.

Centinel asked,

"If [We,] the people are sovereign, how does the opinion of citizens direct the policies of government?"

Jenson wrote,

"The Federalists adopted a theory of the sovereignty of the people in the name of the people, erected a nationalistic government whose purpose was to thwart the will of the [We the] people in whose name they act." (Jensen, Merrill, The Articles of Confederation: An Interpretation of the Social-Constitutional History of the American Revolution, 1774-1781. University of Wisconsin Press, 1959.).

The rules of Madison's Constitution may be unjust, or unwise, but from the perspective of the ruling class consciousness, the Constitution would be better, for them, than the state sovereignty of the Articles of Confederation.

James Wilson, a Federalist, said during the
Philadelphia Convention in 1787 that,

"Laws [in the Constitution] may be unjust,
may be unwise, may be dangerous, may be
destructive; and yet not be so
unconstitutional as to justify the Judges in
refusing to give them effect. But with
regard to every law, however unjust,
oppressive or pernicious, which did not
come plainly under this description, they
would be under the necessity as judges to
give it a free course."

The 38 delegates who signed the document
on September 17, 1787 knew it was a
defective document, and many of the
delegates predicted that Madison's rules
would lead to civil war over the unresolved
issue of slavery.

But, at the time, from the perspective of
the social class awareness of the American
natural aristocracy, the document was
better, for them, than the Articles of
Confederation.

Ben Franklin said, on the last day of the
convention,

"Sir, I agree to this Constitution with all its
faults, if they are such; because I think a
general Government necessary for us,

[natural aristocracy] and there is no form of Government but what may be a blessing to the people if well administered, and believe farther that this is likely to be well administered for a course of years, and can only end in Despotism, as other forms have done before it, when the people shall become so corrupted as to need despotic Government, being incapable of any other. I doubt too whether any other Convention we [ruling class] can obtain may be able to make a better Constitution. For when you assemble a number of men [ruling class] to have the advantage of their joint wisdom, you inevitably assemble with those men, all their prejudices, their passions, their errors of opinion, their local interests, and their selfish views. From such an Assembly can a perfect production be expected?"

Madison argued that the Articles of Confederation had been created by the 13 states, while his new constitution was created by "We the People."

Madison wrote,

"Should all the states adopt it, it will be then a government established by the thirteen states of America, not through the intervention of the legislatures, but by the people at large. In this particular respect the distinction between the existing and the proposed governments is very material. The existing system (The Articles), has been derived from the dependent derivative authority of the legislatures of the states; whereas, this is derived from the superior power of the people."

The rules for ratification by conventions, and not legislatures, would allow the elites, as Madison stated, to obtain ratification

"over the whole body of the people."

As explained by Martin, the ratification process would fail, unless common citizens were, "hurried into it by surprise."

In other words, Morris disclosed that Madison's entire ratification process was designed to gain illegitimate approval in a procedure under the control of the elites in each state.

Morris thought the elites in each state should do whatever they wanted to do to obtain fake ratification.

King responded that the amendment not to seek state legislative approval was equivalent to giving up on a legitimate ratification process.

From Madison's notes,

Mr. L. MARTIN believed Mr. MORRIS to be right, that after a while the people would be against it; but for a different reason from that alleged [by George Mason].. He believed they [common citizens] would not ratify it, unless hurried into it by surprise.

Article 21, as amended, was then agreed to by all the States, Maryland excepted, and Mr. JENIFER being aye.

Article 22 was then taken up, to wit: "This Constitution shall be laid before the United States in Congress assembled, for their approbation; and it is the opinion of this Convention that it should be afterwards submitted to a Convention chosen in each State, under the recommendation of its Legislature, in order to receive the ratification of such Convention."

Mr. GOUVERNEUR MORRIS and Mr. PINCKNEY moved to strike out the words, "for their approbation."

Having dealt with the ratification method, the delegates then turned to the thorny issue of how to handle the evidence of the notes and official minutes of their deliberations

From Madison's notes, September 17, the last day of the Convention.

Mr. KING suggested that the Journals of the Convention should be either destroyed, or deposited in the custody of the President.

He thought, if suffered to be made public, a bad use would be made of them by those who would wish to prevent the adoption of the Constitution. [the anti-federalists.].

Mr. WILSON preferred the second expedient. [given to George Washington for safe keeping]. He had at one time liked the first best; [destroying the official records] but as false suggestions [by George Mason] may be propagated, it should not be made impossible to contradict them [if the records had been destroyed]..

A question was then put on depositing the Journals, and other papers of the Convention, in the hands of the President; on which, — New Hampshire, Massachusetts, Connecticut, New Jersey, Pennsylvania, Delaware, Virginia, North Carolina, South Carolina, Georgia, aye, — 10; Maryland,4 no, — 1.

The President, having asked what the Convention meant should be done with the Journals, &c., whether copies were to be allowed to the members, if applied for, it was resolved, nem. con. "that he retain the Journal and other papers, subject to the order of Congress, if ever formed under the Constitution."

The official Journal notes, of the Convention given to Washington, were buried from public view, and kept in secret, for 20 years, after 1787.

The official notes were finally resurrected in 1818, when John Quincy Adams organized the notes for public distribution, by Max Farrand, published in 1911, about 135 years, after the Convention. (Max Farrand's The Records of the Federal Convention of 1787. Published in 1911.).

As noted in the official government records of the Convention, the Farrand records and notes are now available on the internet, (https://memory.loc.gov/ammem/amlaw/lwfr.html).

From Farrand.

"Accordingly the secretary, William Jackson, after destroying, "all the loose scraps of paper", which he evidently thought unimportant, formally delivered the papers to the president."

Washington in turn, 9 years later, deposited these papers with the Department of State in 1796, where they remained untouched until a resolution by Congress, in 1818, ordered them to be printed.

President Monroe requested the Secretary of State, John Quincy Adams, to take charge of the publication of the Journal.

In addition to the Farrand records, Madison's own notes were kept secret by Madison, until 4 years after his death in 1836.

A limited public distribution of Madison's notes occurred in 1840, after many years of revision by Madison, before he died, to get his version of events the way he wanted them to be seen in public.

Madison had been asked, in 1818, by John Quincy Adams, then Secretary of State, to turn over his notes for public distribution.

Madison had refused. He said that he did not want them to be used in public debates then ongoing over the powers of the judiciary and whether and how to limit slavery.

In summary, Madison conducted the Convention in secret, and the official Journal and Madison's notes were kept in secret for decades after the Convention.

In Jefferson's second observation about self-rule, citizens are deemed irrational and must be kept in a state of "structural ignorance."

Keeping the notes and journal of the Convention in secret from the citizens so that they could not determine Madison's intent to re-impose the British mixed government model is an example of citizen structural ignorance of Madison's unbalanced rules.

Just prior to the vote to approve the text of Madison's Constitution, on September 15, 1787, Madison inserted the language and sanctions against free states that did not return slaves to their owners.

From Madison's notes,

September 15. Took up Article IV, Section 2 (Fugitive Slave clause): Struck out "no person legally held to service or labor in one state escaping into another" and replaced it with "no person held to service or labor in one state, under the laws thereof, escaping to another state."

There was no discussion and no debate about the fugitive slave clause, before the final vote was taken, later that same day.

The other delegates had never seen this text about slavery.

In Madison's conception, individual liberty and equal rights were not a financial "faction," worthy of legal status in the constitution, in the same sense that the working class and the elites were competitive social class factions.

The end goal for Madison was a stable social system, based upon his separation of factions, which would allow the elites to negotiate the spoils of the system with other elites, without including the common citizen faction in the negotiations.

In Federalist #68, Madison explained how defined executive powers would be limited in the new U.S. Constitution:

"unless these departments be so far connected and blended, as to give to each a constitutional control over the others, the degree of separation...essential to a free government can never in practice be duly maintained."

The natural rights anti-federalists correctly pointed out, in 1788, that Madison's separation of power and his Supremacy Clause in Article III, was all about the elite being able to obtain their interest payments on the war bonds in gold and silver, and not in paper money, issued by the states.

Madison and Hamilton needed to find a way to eliminate the power of the states to issue money, and to make the U. S. judiciary the "supreme" power to enforce the provisions of the Constitution over the various state courts.

As Madison wrote in Federalist #48,

"It is agreed on all sides, that the powers properly belonging to one of the departments, ought not to be directly and compleatly administered by either of the other departments. It is equally evident, that neither of them ought to possess directly or indirectly, an overruling influence over the others in the administration of their respective powers."

In An Economic Interpretation of the Constitution of the United States, Charles Beard explained that, for Madison,

"The primary objective of [Madison's] government is the making of rules which determine the property relations of members of society, the dominant classes whose rights are thus to be determined perforce obtain from government."

As noted above in the commentary about Mark Levin's proposed 10 amendments, the second method of amendment has never been successfully implemented.

Madison wrote,

"I do conceive that the constitution may be amended; that is to say, if all power is subject to abuse, that then it is possible the abuse of the powers of the General Government may be guarded against in a more secure manner than is now done, while no one advantage arising from the exercise of that power shall be damaged or endangered by it…(the amendments can be adopted) without endangering any part of the constitution, which is considered as essential to the existence of the Government by those who promoted its adoption."

Madison cited North Carolina's opposition to the Constitution as his motive for including the Bill of Rights.

Madison wrote:

"I allude in a particular manner to those two States that have not thought fit to throw themselves into the bosom of the Confederacy. It is a desirable thing, on our part as well as theirs, that a re-union should take place as soon as possible. I have no doubt, if we proceed to take those steps which would be prudent and requisite at this juncture, [adding 10 amendments] that in a short time we should see that disposition prevailing in those States which have not come in, that we have seen prevailing in those States which have embraced the constitution."

In his argument with George Mason about the difficulty of amending the Constitution, or adding a Bill of Rights, Madison's argument hinged on deleting the term "expressly delegated" in the Articles of Confederation.

After Madison had drafted the Bill of Rights, he deleted the term "expressly delegated," in the 10th amendment.

In the absence of the phrase "expressly delegated, Supreme Court Justice Marshall could rule in Madison v. McCullough, that the Federal government had unlimited, implied powers.

Marshall ruled,

"Among the enumerated powers, we do not find that of establishing a bank or creating a corporation. But there is no phrase in the instrument which, like the Articles of Confederation, excludes incidental or implied powers and which requires that everything granted shall be expressly and minutely described. Even the 10th Amendment, which was framed for the purpose of quieting the excessive jealousies which had been excited, omits the word "expressly," and declares only that the powers "not delegated to the United States, nor prohibited to the States, are reserved to the States or to the people," thus leaving the question whether the particular power which may become the subject of contest has been delegated to the one Government, or prohibited to the other."

Consequently, the implied powers, not cited in the Constitution, but not "expressly prohibited," in Article 10, granted the government the authority to charter Hamilton's First Bank, and for both agencies of the Federal Government and private citizens to own stock in the bank, along with foreign investors.

Marshall wrote,

"The bill for incorporating the Bank of the United States did not steal upon an unsuspecting legislature and pass unobserved. Its principle was completely understood, and was opposed with equal zeal and ability. After being resisted first in the fair and open field of debate, and afterwards in the executive cabinet, [Jefferson] with as much persevering talent as any measure has ever experienced, and being supported by arguments which convinced minds as pure and as intelligent as this country can boast, it became a law…it is the unanimous and decided opinion of this Court that the act to incorporate the Bank of the United States is a law made in pursuance of the Constitution, and is a part of the supreme law of the land."

James Buchanan writes that analysis and evaluation of constitutional rules is a two-step process.

In the first step, the rules of the Constitution are created which are like the rules of a game.

After the Constitution has been ratified, citizens engage in economic market competition, based upon the rules of the game.

Referees, or in the government's case, judges, determine if rules have been violated during competition.

As written by Wilenz,

"Hamilton's fiscal plan would, he believed, ally the federal government to a particular class of speculators, create (through the national bank) a means to dispense political bounties to political favorites and bribes to opponents and introduce what Madison called the "corrupt influence" of substituting the motive of private interests in place of the public duty."

Based upon Marshall's decision on the Federal Government's implied powers, what Hamilton and Madison succeeded in creating was the old form of tyranny, where a powerful minority of elites, as a collectivist class, rule over politically powerless individuals, whose interests are subordinated to those on the top.

In re-imposing the British mixed government social class system, in 1787, Madison denied the possibility that common American citizens would ever have a common set of constitutional moral values, because his rules spread the interests of the common citizens across election districts in various states, in contrast to Montesquieu's dictum of the coherency of cultural values in a small republic.

Once the elected representatives in Madison's constitution arrive in Washington, they find that the purpose of Madison's rules are to balance the financial interests of one class against the other, not secure the rights of citizens.

In Madison's centralized representative republic, the representatives represent their social class financial interests.

Following Buchanan, the financial interests that they represent are their own personal financial interests because protecting common citizen liberty was not the purpose of government.

Under Madison's social class conflict model of government, liberty would have required its own political party.

Liberty would be seen as just another special interest, like the financial interests of the natural aristocracy, to be balanced and separated, just like other special financial interest.

This is the lesson of the Agrarians, cited above, when they attempted to form a new political party.

Liberty, under Madison's two-party system, does not have a political party.

"The reason," noted John Adams, why liberty does not have its own political party is,

"that we have no Americans in America. The Federalists have been no more Americans than the anties...Jefferson had a party. Hamilton had a party, but the commonwealth [liberty] had none."

The key concern of Madison was that the majority of common citizens would form a political social class consciousness, as the common citizens in England already had, and that common citizens would use the agencies of government to oppress the minority of wealthy elites.

Madison called this oppression of common citizen majority rule, "tyranny."

The solution, for Madison, was permanently loading the constitutional rules against common citizens participating in the decisions of government.

The true distinction of the American system, wrote Madison in Federalist #71,

"lies in the total exclusion of the people, in their collective capacity in any share in the government."

In America's current two party special interest spoils system, the political elites are not bound by the same rules that are imposed upon the non-elite.

The natural aristocracy has a coherent social class consciousness that guides their plunder of the system.

The middle and working classes in America do not have a comparable social class consciousness, and are powerless, under Madison's rules, to amend or reform his system.

When the Marxist Democrats subverted the election system, in 2020, in order to steal an election, Madison's flawed constitution contained no remedy by common citizens for this outcome because his rendition of the British mixed system was defective.

The U. S. Supreme Court refused to hear the Texas complaint in a case of original jurisdiction, allowing the election corruption to pass unchallenged by the Supreme Law of the land.

Madison's contemporary natural aristocracy are beyond the rule of law, when they engage in corruption.

They operate above the law, with no consequences for rule breaking.

Only the common citizens are subjected to the rule of law, given to them by the elites who make and enforce the law.

The term Marxist Democrats use to describe this form of oligarchy is "Our democracy."

The word "our," is accurate. It refers to the exclusive power of the ruling class version of government power.

The government Madison created is the government of the wealthy.

Madison's government is not the government by the people, for the people, and of the people.

In an odd ironic twist of history, Madison's preoccupation with mob rule of common citizens turned out to be criminal mob rule by the natural aristocracy.

From a philosophical point of view, the "mob-rule" of the Biden family and the Clintons, would not have happened, if, in 1787, the American constitution had been written to give citizens more structural political power to protect and preserve their natural rights.

Reclaiming the American Democratic Impulse means re-asserting Jefferson's cultural moral priority of individual citizen liberty as the mission of government, based upon the principle that citizens are fully capable to engage in self-government.

Chapter 5. The Emergence of A Stable Middle Class Economic Social Order.

Adam Smith, in The Wealth and Poverty of Nations, (1776), identified seven social/institutional variables that, historically, seemed to contribute to the wealth of nations.

These variables were:
- private property rights,
- individual civil rights,
- legal rights of contract,
- consistently stable institutions of government with peaceful measures for the transfer of power,
- institutions of government that respond to the petitions of citizens,
- honest government whose leaders and bureaucrats do not lie to citizens, and
- efficient government that makes no large claims on the incomes of citizens.

Smith claimed that when national economies exhibited these characteristics that,

"As every individual, therefore, endeavours as much as he can both to employ his capital in the support of domestic industry, and so to direct that industry that its produce may be of the greatest value; every individual necessarily labours to render the annual revenue of the society as great as he can. He generally, indeed, neither intends to promote the public interest, nor knows how much he is promoting it. By preferring the support of domestic to that of foreign industry, he intends only his own security; and by directing that industry in such a manner as its produce may be of the greatest value, he intends only his own gain, and he is in this, as in many other cases, led by an invisible hand to promote an end which was no part of his intention. Nor is it always the worse for the society that it was no part of it. By pursuing his own interest he frequently promotes that of the society more effectually than when he really intends to promote it." (Book 4, Chapter 2.).

The passage from Smith identifies the national sovereign interest as the macro economic goal that would be improved by individual initiative.

In Smith's theory, the force of individual economic self-interest was linked, in a beneficial way, to improvements in the welfare of society.

The major question Smith was asking was how a nation, as a national sovereign economic entity, could achieve the greatest wealth.

Smith's observations addressed aggregate national wealth, not the distribution of wealth among different classes of citizens, or the institutional distribution of political power required to bring about free market exchanges.

When the seven characteristics of the society were present in a sovereign nation, then Smith predicted that a stable economic social order would emerge as a result of autonomous free market exchange.

In contrast to Hobbes, who thought that Leviathan was required for a stable social order, or Madison, who thought that a stable social order could only be achieved by rule of the elites, Smith offered an entirely unique perspective that social stability would emerge as a result of autonomous exchanges in the competitive free market.

However, in order for social stability to emerge as a result of free market exchanges, each individual depends upon the other party to follow the civil rules of justice.

This dependency on another to follow rules establishes the condition of social voluntary obedience to the rules.

When all citizens follow the rules, there is equality before the law in voluntary rule obedience, which creates social stability.

The philosophical link between Smith's "invisible hand," in free market exchange, and equality before the law is that the free market provides each citizen with a path to prosperity through individual initiative.

When all citizens have the economic freedom to pursue prosperity, the emergence of a stable social system is a result of free market exchanges.

To quote Smith again, in this system of natural liberty,

"Every man, as long as he does not violate the laws of justice, is left perfectly free to pursue his own interest in his own way, and to bring both his industry and capital into competition with those of any other man, or order of men" (Smith, 1776.).

In an article titled "The Justice of Natural Liberty," Buchanan quotes this passage from Smith:

"To hurt in any degree the interest of any one order of citizens for no other purpose but to promote that of some other, is evidently contrary to that justice and equality of treatment which the sovereign owes to all different orders of his subjects." (1976.).

Market exchanges are the institutional mechanism through which individuals derive freedom of choice and economic opportunity, without the constraint of ruling class coercion or exploitation.

In contrast, political exchanges are defined by a constitution, where the primary values being exchanged are aimed at how individuals treat each other in on-going legal transactions over the entire life of the individual.

In the case of political equilibrium, the system is stable, meaning there are relatively few riots and assassinations during the periods of power transfer from one special interest group to the other.

Political equilibrium, not individual economic freedom, becomes the end of

Madison's rules, to which society is directed by competition in the political system between financial factions.

Free market exchange provides the adhesive glue that binds individuals to follow the rule of law because universal rule obedience is a necessary ingredient for all citizens to achieve economic prosperity.

The moral value of the market lies in its ability to create opportunities for the individual to fulfill her destiny.

Free market exchange becomes a means to facilitate individual freedom, not a constitutional public purpose, in and of itself.

Freedom is secured when a constitution establishes a moral contract between individuals that defends freedom, in conjunction with ambient cultural values that reinforce the moral obligations entailed in the civil defense of freedom for the entire society.

Political equilibrium, as a constitutional concept in Madison's rules, has no adhesive glue that binds individuals to defending each other freedoms in the current period, and does not have adhesive power for generating loyalty to the political system in future generations.

In Madison's rules, the elites follow a different set of economic exchange rules than the common citizens because the elites derive unelected legal power to use the agencies of government to promote their own welfare.

In other words, economic exchange, alone, in Madison's rules, do not promote voluntary allegiance for all citizens to follow the rules.

James Buchanan, in The Reason of Rules, and Constitutional Economics, described one of Madison's flaws when he addressed the notion that politicians have welfare functions that are different from the collectivist groups they purport to represent. (Buchanan, James M., The Reason of Rules: Constitutional Political Economy (The Collected Works of James M. Buchanan,) Liberty Fund, 2000.).

The welfare function that politicians maximize is their own individual function, not some undefined general social welfare function such as "in order to form a more perfect union."

Madison substituted the priority of ruling class welfare for Jefferson's equal freedom, as if the welfare function of the ruling class served as the social welfare function of all citizens. [We, the people].

Morality in market exchanges become an issue of public concern, in Madison's rules, whenever fate control involving coercion, manipulation and subjugation occurs, after the constitutional rules had been established.

The constitutional public interest priority of liberty would be especially high in cases of market exchange where an oppressed individual has no means of escape from the exchange relationship.

The threat to individual freedom arises because one party, the natural aristocracy, has the ability to subjugate the sovereign life path of the less powerful party, the common citizens.

Following Adam Smith, the benefits of economic growth, in a free market, are diffused through society, and do not accrue solely to the agent that made the capital investment or used specialized skills to produce a product.

The national economic effect of economic growth is to push the national production possibility frontier outward without the negative equilibrium effects on incomes, prices, interest rates, or investment opportunities, in a zero-sum economy.

National economic growth is an unambiguous social and economic good in a free market because the benefits of economic growth are distributed to all social classes.

Economic growth creates new future opportunities for individuals to achieve control over their destiny.

The wide social distribution of the benefits of growth are secured in a constitutional contract of equal rights for all and special privileges for none.

Future economic growth, in free market exchange, contributes to the individual's control over the individual's sovereign destiny.

When there is no economic growth in the special interest system, the status quo does not change, and the loser groups never recover from their subjugation in the absence of economic opportunity.

That cultural value orientation of individual freedom that results from wide-spread benefits of economic growth is counter to the group collectivist value orientation of either contemporary socialist group welfare or the ruling class collectivist values resulting from the evolution of Madison's special interest political system.

Allowing individuals the greatest freedom to pursue their destiny is the only unambiguous constitutional public purpose that would bind every individual to serving the public purpose.

The attainment of that constitutional public purpose is served when the sovereign national economy experiences sustained economic growth.

Serving the public purpose provides the logical justification for establishing the priority of improvement of individual welfare as the key unit of analysis in the political system that ensues from the constitutional democratic framework.

One of the outcomes of establishing the priority of individual freedom as the telos of the constitution is that equal civil rights achieves a higher ranking than property rights in the hierarchy of constitutional rights.

This establishment of superior individual rights is a necessary first step in untangling the conflicting set of cultural values between elites and common citizens that has evolved since the time of Madison and Hamilton.

In constitutional rule making, when citizens leave the imaginary state of nature, a majority of individuals imagine that a rule or regulation leads to greater freedom for themselves, and that the rule would affect the freedom of others in a like manner.

If a majority of citizens imagine this universal rule, the rule would be adopted, and citizens who gave the rule to themselves share a moral obligation to obey the law that they had given themselves.

John Stuart Mill suggested that the constitutional structure or form of government for any given society was amenable to choice by the citizens of the society.

In his essay on representative government, Mill asked:

"...by what test the choice should be directed; what are the distinctive characteristics of the form of government best fitted to promote the interests of any given society?" (Utilitarianism, Liberty, and Representative Government, 1863.).

Mill is asking two questions, a primary question of what constitutes the constitutional public purpose, and flowing from that question, what form or structure of constitutional institutions promote the attainment of that public purpose, after the constitution has been implemented.

If the public purpose is defined by the highest priority of individual freedom, for example, then what form of institutions would the citizens choose?

The reason for Mill's initial emphasis on the definition of the constitutional public purpose relates to how the ensuing power of government is used through the creation of subsequent institutions.

A constitutional structure, given Mill's emphasis, can provide for economic institutions that offer citizens opportunities to come into contact with other citizens to determine joint sovereignty.

Given the emphasis on citizen obedience to follow rules, a structure of government institutions can be created that promote citizen forums for the exchange of values.

For Mill, and for Jefferson, there exists a unique constellation of cultural ethical values that facilitate the development of individual morality that Mills calls virtue.

In suggesting that the initial constitutional structure was open to citizen choice, Mill assumed, like Jefferson, that the unifying principles that motivate individuals to form a constitution were self-evident.

For Mill, the motivation to enter a constitutional relationship required that individual freedom serve as the public purpose.

Freedom, as the public purpose, requires a certain type of social and cultural value orientation to sustain obedience to the constitutional structure that individuals choose to create.

In Constitutional Economics. Buchanan makes the assumption that individuals are rational in the pursuit of their own sovereign life mission.

Buchanan relies on a philosophy of logic to explain how the end goals, clearly stated in a constitution, create the binding allegiance for citizens to follow the rules of the game.

In other words, rather than relying on the separation of powers to deal with the problem of special interests, as Madison did, Buchanan relies upon the rationality of self-interest as a force that binds individuals to society as a process of rationally minimizing risk in uncertain decision making environments.

In leaving the state of nature, and forming a constitution, individual citizens are placed in a position of uncertainty in the outcome of their life's mission.
No individual knows in advance where the individual may end up, given the choice between one set of constitutional rules or another.

A rational individual, with a rational self-interest, would choose fair rules for all, aimed at the greatest freedom for all.

In constitutional decision-making under uncertainty, individuals would seek rules that had maximum equal rights for all, with special privileges for none.

The end goal, or telos, of the constitution, in this case of rational self-interest, is individual freedom.

In the presence of uncertainty over future reciprocity and mutual obligation, as ther is in Madison's framework, there will be more short term calculation on breaking social rules, and an emphasis on short term financial gains.

In the presence of uncertainty over the rules of justice, social exchanges resemble zero sum relationships that more closely approximate the special interest elitist system that emphasizes the distribution of wealth from a corrupt political and legal system.

Buchanan saw the market mechanism as the force for the emergence of a stable social order in which individuals cooperate for the mutual gain of all who engage in voluntary exchanges.

In The Calculus of Consent, Buchanan and Tullock write,

"If property rights are carefully defined, should not the pure laissez-faire [laissez passer] organization bring about the elimination of all significant externalities? … After human and property right are initially defined, will externalities that are serious enough to warrant removing really be present? Or will voluntary co-operative arrangements among individuals emerge to insure the elimination of all relevant external effects? (Buchanan, James, M., and Tullock, Gordon, The Calculus of Consent: Logical Foundations for Constitutional Democracy, The University of Michigan Press, 1962.).

By allowing individuals the liberty to make their own choices, and by enabling them to cooperate with others to achieve their goals, individuals are best able to improve their own welfare while not infringing on the liberty of others to do likewise

Buchanan believed that individuals want to make their own life and financial choices. They do not want others to tell them what to do with their lives.

The social contract, as Buchanan viewed it, is the set of rules and constraints to which everyone would agree was better than the state of nature.

Constitutional rules are constraints that we impose on ourselves, as distinct from limits on the availability of economic resources and other such constraints that are imposed on us by nature.

In setting the constraints, the citizens agree that whatever gains arise from the changes from leaving the state of nature are shared by all citizens.

Individuals choose to impose constraints or limits on their own behavior as a part of an exchange in which the restrictions on their own actions are sacrificed in return for the benefits that are anticipated from the reciprocally extended restrictions on the actions of others.

After the constitutional rules have been implemented, then the citizens choose the set of government institutions that will enforce the constraints on all citizens, otherwise known as the equal application of the law.

Institutions, defined broadly, are variables subject to deliberative evaluation and to explicit choice. (Buchanan and Tullock, 1962.).

In agreeing to be governed, explicitly or implicitly, the individual exchanges his own liberty with others who similarly give up liberties in exchange for the benefits offered by a regime characterized by behavioral limits.

In the individualist philosophy of Buchanan, the state is not an agency existing independently of citizens.

The state has no greater knowledge than is possessed by its citizens. Nor is the state or the officials chosen to execute this process the eqal application of the lawdriven by motives more benevolent than are the motives that drive the self-interested citizens who bargain with each other to create the judicial institutions of the state

Neither the state, nor society, is a singular and sentient creature capable of making choices about the welfare of individual citizens.

Because there is no such thing as Rousseau's general will or group social welfare beyond the aggregation of welfare of each of the individuals in the society, the democratic political institutions created, after the constitution is implemented, reflect the preferences of the citizens as closely as possible.

Reclaiming the American democratic impulse means re-asserting the philosophy that free market exchange, in a constitution of citizen liberty, leads to the emergence of a stable social order that is superior to the collectivist vision of Madison' ruling class, or to the totalitarian socialist social order of modern day Marxists.

Chapter 6. Reclaiming The American Democratic Impulse.

Reclaiming the American democratic impulse means replacing Madison's British mixed social class competition model of government with the original American Spirit of Liberty that the patriots adopted in their fight with King George.

There are certain components of the American democratic impulse that can be reclaimed and updated in a new constitution that establishes individual liberty as the mission of the new constitution.

Reclaiming the American democratic impulse is based upon the definition of the purpose of government held by the Populists, as described by Richard Tuck, in Natural Rights Theories: Their Origins and Development.

He wrote that the Populists believed that,

"Government was a trust, set up to serve the interests of the governed, and was best achieved by making the interests of the governed and governors identical. The public interest is the honoring of the trust that is government, that the interest of each is the interest of all. Perfectly rational beings would devote themselves to the public good so understood." (Tuck, Richard, Natural Rights Theories: Their Origins and Development, Cambridge University Press, 1979.).

Initially, the Populists assumed that everyone in America shared this belief about the purpose of government.

Their first political efforts at reform were based upon the idea that if everyone shared this idea, that they could just insert "good people" who had the right set of cultural values, into the existing political system, and reform would be forthcoming.

According to Bruce Palmer, in Man Over Money,

"The Southern populists did not realize that the government was not designed to serve the purposes of the farmers or the laborers or of any kind of radical reformers."

In its modern application, this principle would be stated that the purpose of government is to secure the equal rights of citizens and to promote the national sovereignty in foreign affairs.

The public purpose is obtained when citizen's rights are secure and the purpose of government is to extend the freedom of individual citizens.

Following the ideas of the Populists, a constitution that set the rules for a constitutional democratic republic would be based upon the following principles:

Individual Self Interest.

Political governance must be based on an appeal to the individual's self-interest, based upon improving the individual's control over the individual's economic destiny.

V. O. Key noted that the system of economic and political apartheid imposed on the South by the Democrats was not simply about "white supremacy."

He said,

"the issue of Negro suffrage is a question not of white supremacy but the supremacy of which whites."

The constitutional system of special interests created by Madison enabled this ruling class political arrangement and allowed it to function unchallenged because the constitution was silent on how individual self-interest served the public purpose.

This difference in interpretation about the role of individual self-interest was eloquently expressed by the North Carolina Bourbon Democratic Supreme Court jurist, Thomas Ruffin, in 1866.

"The natural rights," said Ruffin,

"inherent in freedom, entitled people to security in person and property under the law; but political rights were 'conventional' not 'natural' because they involved powers over the Constitution and laws and were granted according to the sense of the community of the fitness of particular classes."

Ruffin, just like Madison and Hamilton 100 years before, believed that only a certain segment of society was fit to govern.

When the constitutional rules flowed over into what Ruffin called "conventional" or commercial rules, then only a certain segment of the society were fit to make decisions about other individual's self interest.

Agrarian opponents of the Democrats understood exactly where this anti-democratic philosophy would lead.

According to an 1868 editorial in the Randolph Sun,

"Democrats say the ignorant people are not fit to choose their own officers. Is that right? No, it involves a principle of tyranny and oppression."

Under one set of cultural values, individual natural rights extended to political andconstitutional rights.

As captured by Jefferson, these values were,

"...to maintain the will for the majority of the convention and of the people themselves. We believed, with them, that man was a rational animal, endowed by nature with rights and an innate sense of justice: and that he could be restrained from wrong and protected in right, by moderate powers, confided to persons of his own choice and held to their duties by dependence on his own will."

The set of cultural values associated with the notion that certain people are unfit to govern leads not only to tyranny, but to a centralization of power, a trend easily seen by de Tocqueville as early as 1832.

He concluded that "statism" was the promise of American life leading to a "concentration of power and the subjection of individuals..."

Albert Bushnell Hart, in his 1910 book, The Southern South, that,

"southerners lived under a rigid hierarchy of elite domination: in no other region did a small aristocracy exercise such prestige and influence...in the South, the well-to-do, the cultured, the educated and the well connected absolutely controlled society." (Hart, Albert Bushnell, The Southern South, New York, D. Appleton and Company, 1910.).

As noted by the editorial in the Democratic newspaper, The Wilmington Post, on April 26, 1878,

"If the colored people will trust us, and vote with us, we will act in their interests, just as we do for the interests of the women and minors, who do not vote at all." Translated into action, what the Democrats did next was take away the rights of black people to vote, just like the women and minors, who did not vote at all."

The constitutional principle of individualism is based upon Jefferson's

notion that every person has an innate, natural right to self-rule.

Individual Equal Rights.

In 1882, a former plantation owner was quoted in Steven Hahn's book, The Roots of Southern Populism, as saying,

"There is no principle involved in politics since the Civil War. It is only a contest between the ins and the outs for place and power and for the privilege and opportunity to rob the U. S. Treasury." (Hahn, Steven, The Roots of Southern Populism: Yeomen Farmers and the Transformation of the Georgia Upcountry, 1850-1890, Oxford University Press, 1983.).

The good people inserted into politics by the farmers, who were not initially interested in robbing the treasury, were soon corrupted by the political system.

After some period of time elapsed, the leaders of the Populist movement became as interested in robbing the treasury as the elite special interests.

When equal individual rights are not the primary goal of political ideology, the outcome predicted by John Adams, of a

national society divided between the wealthy and the poor, is inevitable.

John Bassett, a keen observer and critic of North Carolina's Bourbon Democrats, noted that the tactics of the Democrats taught the farmers an important political lesson. The election, (of 1899) said Bassett, is

"one more step in the educating of our people that it is right to lie, to steal, and to defy all honesty in order to keep a certain party in power." (Bassett, John Spencer, Slavery in the State of North Carolina, Johns Hopkins Press, 1899.).

Leonidas Polk mentioned equal rights in one of his speeches about the Democrats, when he asked how long it would take for the values surrounding equal rights to be embraced and implemented in the political system.

"How long will it take?...Not long, because no lie can live forever. How long?...Not long because the arm of the moral universe is long, but it bends toward justice."

The lie Polk referred to was that ordinary Americans could to be denied equal rights by the elites over a long period of time.

Polk was wrong about his assessment of how long it would take for the principle of equal rights to take hold because the constitution of Madison contained no mechanism for common citizens to reclaim their rights, once the constitution was enacted in sham ratification conventions.

Open and Fair Political Participation.

The individual farmers thought that they could benefit from a mass social movement aimed at gaining control over the economic forces that controlled the debt peonage system.

As long as the tenant farmers thought that the movement was headed in a direction that improved economic control, they supported the broader political goals of the agrarian movement.

A constitution that aims at greater citizen control over government must continually allow maximum citizen participation in the development and enforcement of rules over political policies.

Schwartz noted that the farmer's interests could not,

"...be dependent on, or embedded in, the original system, [Madison's system] since that system is based on the exercise of routinized power by the dominant groups. A threat to the continuing functioning of a system cannot be mounted by the system itself." (Schwartz, 1978).

Schwartz writes about the disconnect that arose between the leaders of the Populist Party and the members.

The leadership of the Populists began to,

"...suppress information, suspend democratic decision making and impose a policy that benefited only a small minority."

The farmers were initially attracted to the Populist Party because the leaders had created an economic alternative to the merchant-banker crop lien system.

This alternative economic structure appealed to the farmer's urge for economic self control.

According to Schwartz,

"...when the (Democrat) banks attacked, and when the newspaper stories questioned the Exchange's economic viability, the farmer's treated the Exchange just like any other merchant: They began to shop elsewhere."

In other words, they went back to the Democratic Party, and then stayed there for another 100 years.

Imposing Citizen Limits on the Federal Government.

In his article, "The Ninth Amendment and Contemporary Jurisprudence," Edward Erler noted that,

"constitutional government means that the people retain the mass of sovereign power and delegate only certain portions of that sovereignty in the form of enumerated powers to government."

The decisions of the majority in this constitutional arrangement are legitimate to the extent that they are directed to the larger philosophical goals of individual freedom, undergirded by allegiance to the rule of law.

The direction of reform is towards a representative democratic republic that empowers citizens to use the Ninth Amendment as a guide to limit the power and authority of the Federal Government from direct operation on the individual rights and freedoms of citizens.

Limiting Taxes, Government Debt and Government Spending.

In Economic Origins of Jeffersonian Democracy, Charles Beard writes that Federalists, in 1789, promoted the new constitution by stating that,

"...the new government was to restore public credit, establish adequate revenues, create a nation-wide judicial system, pay the debt strengthen the defense on land and sea, and afford adequate support to trade and commerce."(Beard, Charles Austin, The Economic Origins of Jeffersonian Democracy, New York, Macmillan Co., 1915.).

Nothing in Madison's constitution served to check or balance how much the federal government could tax or spend, even though Madison's notes showed that the topic was debated extensively.

As noted by Lefler and Newsome in North Carolina: The History of A Southern State,

"The Democrats adopted the policy of stimulating railroad, industrial, mercantile, and banking development by unrestrictive private enterprise protected and aided by the state government." (Lefler, Hugh Talmage, Newsome, Albert R., North Carolina: The History of A Southern State, UNC Press, 1973.).

They used tax revenues and government spending to their own financial advantage, all the while maintaining politically that

they were the special friends of black people and common whites.

"Thus, until after 1900," writes Lefler and Newsome,

"the industrialists succeeded in rebuffing efforts at state regulation, in wresting huge profits from labor, and the consuming public, and in preserving the fiction that the interests of the manufacturers, labor, and the public were identical and not conflicting."

The citizens have the right to restrict the rate of taxation and government spending to limits of population growth, with modification to rates of taxation only by a 2/3 vote of the citizens.

Clean and Fair Elections, Fair Re-Districting and Competitive Elections.

When the state delegates from Mecklinburg County were sent to North Carolina's first state constitutional convention, in 1776, the citizens who elected them gave the delegates specific instructions.

According to Charles Maddry, in The North Carolina Constitution of 1776,

"The delegates were instructed to endeavor to establish a free government under the authority of the people of North Carolina – a simple democracy, the fundamental principles of which should oppose everything leaning toward autocracy or power in the hands of the rich against the poor."

The direction of a citizen's democratic reform would be to assert constitutional authority over the method of redistricting, and the legal oversight of voting procedures and counting of votes.

Voter registration fraud, vote counting fraud, and redistricting fraud are one of the special gifts of Madison's system of special interest corruption, provided by a constitution that is silent on how citizens are supposed to protect citizen's rights.

Citizen Initiatives, Term Limits, Rights of Recall and Referendums on Tax Increases.

Constitutional reform must aim at providing citizens the mechanisms to take power away from the central government, and give it to the states, and to the citizens themselves.

The type of reforms sought would enhance the provisions of the ninth and tenth amendments, which were weak attempts at limiting the power of the central government.

Protecting Private Property Against Appropriation by Government Agents.

Private property is relevant to the creation of the new constitution because of its relationship to an owner's ability to appropriate the fruits of his labor and returns on his investments.

The legitimacy of a claim of private property is related to an economic system of rewards based upon merit and individual achievement.

Following Jefferson, all legitimate authority is derived from the consent of the governed, and claims of private property made by agents of government that are not so derived are illegitimate.

The direction of for creating a new constitution in America begins with the protection of the individual's rights of private property.

Eliminating Government Secrecy and Corporate Welfare Corruption.

The Democrats in Southern states, around 1895, began using the agencies of state government in increasingly elaborate secret schemes to use government revenues to recruit industry to the South.

The new industries would locate on industrial sites and land now owned by the elites, which had been successfully taken away from the farmers in the debt lien system.

As described by Cash,

"What with free sites and waiving of taxes, about all the South was getting out of the removal of the New England mills was the stingy sums paid in wages (to the southern mill workers)...The increased employment was a boon of sorts, perhaps. But a boon purchased at the appalling prices of virtually giving away the inherent resources of the section, physical and human."

The recruitment of low wage, semi-skilled jobs using tax incentives, according to Cash,

"gave away the wealth of the South on a scale hitherto unprecedented in a region which has always too eagerly given away its wealth. And, it exacts no adequate advantage...the people who mainly gain from it are the merchants and bankers."

According to Wood, the State (of North Carolina) is thus a result of the history of class struggle while at the same time a participant in it.

"It (the state government) must secure the conditions necessary for capital accumulation in a context of class conflict and by means that are themselves conditioned by class conflict."

One of the ways the Democrats gave away the state's resources, according to Ayers, in the Promise of the New South, was by continually promising business corporate interests, in secret meetings, that they would not raise corporate income taxes.

"The Democratic promise included low taxes on railroads and farmlands, with few restrictions on business and few demand on government."

One of the 'few restrictions" on business included no restrictions on how young a person could be to work in the mill, nor how long the children could work.

Furthermore, by keeping taxes low, and encouraging child labor at age six, the Democrats did not spend money on the public education system, which at the time, aimed at education of both blacks and whites.

Generally, it is to the advantage of the elite interests to control free flows of information, and to meet in secret to conduct their business.

The constitutional public purpose of individual prosperity is directly linked to open and free flows of information that must be protected.

The direction of the new constitution is to mandate open forums and free flows of information, while outlawing secret meetings, where the public business is conducted.

The rules on public access to public information must be strengthened, and sanctions for violating open meetings and open access should be strictly enforced, by the citizens.

Reliance on Free Market Competition for Creating A Stable Social Order.

As noted by Cash,

"Whatever the intent of the original (New South) founders of progress, the plain truth is that everything here rested finally upon one fact alone: cheap labor...the wages were on average just about adequate to the support of a single individual – such wages as required that every member of a family moving from the land into Factory-town, who was not incapacitated by disease or age or infancy, should go into the mills in order that he too might eat."

What the farmers learned from their experience in the mills, beginning around 1880, was that the purported benefits of the free market system of competition do not work well if there are no rules on fair exchange, not just in wage rates but in all commercial transactions.

The rules and laws must grant ordinary individual citizens rights of standing in court to enforce the rules.

In other words, in contrast to Judge Ruffin's notion that rights did not extend to commercial transactions, the new constitution would make this principle a part of the commercial fabric of the society.

One of the mistakes the farmers and populists made is to assume that fair rules of exchange would be enforced by agents of government.

What they learned is that the agents of government are controlled by the special political interests, who could not care less about enforcement of fair rules on behalf of common citizens.

The constitutional job of the agents of government in Madison's special interest system, is to enforce the status quo benefits of economic and financial power that the special interests derive from their privileged insider positions.

Individual citizens must be equipped with the legal authority and ability to enforce the rules of fair trade and fair exchange, on their own behalf, against the entrenched financial interests who control both political parties.

James Buchanan and Geoffrey Brennan have written extensively on the theory of democracy as it relates to the development of fair economic laws and financial rules.

They emphasize that the development of fair rules is a political process, in contrast to the current socialist emphasis of achieving a desired outcome in the distribution of income among social groups.

In The Reason of Rules, they write that,

"Our specific claim is that justice takes its meaning from the rules for the social order within which notions of justice are to be applied. To appeal to considerations of justice is to appeal to relevant rules."

This interpretation of justice as fair rules is dramatically different than Madison's notion that relies on a set of elites who judge the fairness of welfare outcomes and have the power to shift resources from one social group to another.

Buchanan and Brennan continue by noting,

"To the extent that this (Madison's existing) constitution commands little respect, in part because it is seen to fail in its function of limiting the scope of both governmental and private intrusion into what are widely held to be protected spheres of activity."

The existing constitution allows privileged classes to change the rules as it may suit their needs, and to apply business and economic rules that apply to others, but not to themselves.

The rules of the new constitution would be based upon equality before the law, which would eliminate the ruling class unearned privileges.

Local Government and Local Economies.

A new constitution that aims at promoting greater citizen participation and more citizen control over the affairs of government must first establish a geographical territorial stronghold in local governments.

Leonidas Polk had expressed his interest in the creation of many small, diversified industries in the South. His comments came during the time that farmers in small towns were raising capital to invest in community mills.

Dwight Billings notes that as early as 1828, the North Carolina House of Commons discussed how the state's economy could generate more opportunities for its citizens, while decreasing the economic dependency on outside capital.

One passage from the minutes of that delegation read,

"In setting about to ameliorate our condition the first step is to adopt some system that will enable us to buy less and sell more – that will enable us to supply within ourselves, our own wants and necessities...Instead of sending off at great expense of our transportation, our raw material, convert it into fabrics at home, and in that state, bring it to market...the manufacturing system will become our greatest means of wealth and prosperity: it will change the course of trade, and, in a great measure, make us independent of Europe and the North."

Paul Escott explains that the point of the Democrat's attack on local government was easy to understand.

"It is easy to see why the Democratic offensive was aimed so directly at local government. Control of county affairs had been the foundation of North Carolina's aristocratic social order...In February of

1877, the legislature abolished elected county government and put local power back into the hands of appointed officials."

By centralizing political power in the southern state capitals, the Democrats eliminated the source of strength for farmer's to organize a political opposition party.

According to V. O. Key,

"For a two-party system to operate effectively each party must, almost of necessity, have a territorial stronghold in which it can win legislative elections and control local government. The powers exercised by the central government of Virginia over local officials make it difficult to found an opposition faction or control of local government."

Consumer Fair Trade and Fair Credit.

According to Perlman, in The Road to Redemption,

"...the public debts that were being renounced had been incurred for the very reason that the South did not have any private capital of its own to draw on...it would be forced into utter reliance on outside resources...external capital tended to consolidate and control the southern economy...the South had in effect, surrendered control over its future economic development."

Initially, what the farmers wanted was equal access to capital to make investments in their farms and to finance the next crop.

What they found, according to Stephen Hahn, was a territorial financial monopoly,

"which prevented competition in the extension of credit, and a monopoly over the sources of necessary credit in a system increasingly dominated by staple agriculture."

This last element of monopoly had a handy title of "no cotton, no credit."

The farmer's response to the banker and merchant financial monopoly was to create competitive alternatives in the form of the Agrarian Cooperative Exchanges and Macune's Sub-Treasury system.

These programs tended to open up pathways of occupational mobility for farmers, and thus, constituted a threat to the plantation aristocracy's position of monopoly power.

The monopoly financial power was used to restrain geographical and occupational mobility of the farmers.

The farmers could not obtain credit to finance independent business activities, and could not leave the region in order to get out of debt under the conditions created by the monopoly.

In response to the competitive threat posed by the Populist alternatives, the Democrats counter-attacked.

In 1893, the Democrats in the North Carolina General Assembly changed the state law to make it illegal for the Farmer's Alliance to engage in the credit business of the cooperative.

Then, in 1899, when they took total one-party political control, they permanently eliminated the threat posed by the Populist Party by outlawing alternative forms of credit that their own commercial bankers did not control.

The use of credit and capital by the Democrats to achieve one-party control was based on two weapons:

- restrict the geographical mobility of farmers, through enforcement of merchant liens, and,

- when the farmers lost their lands to the bankers and went into the mills, keep the wages of the white labor force near poverty levels.

That combination created a powerful economic and financial dependency of individuals to support the "Party of their Fathers."

Civic Education: "Giving Every Person A Chance for Making Economic and Social Progress."

In the mid-1880s, when Walter Hines Page established the citizen's educational advocacy group called The Watauga Club, he was quoted as saying,

"North Carolina discourages intellectual aspiration, independent thought and mental growth...There is absolutely no chance for the ambitious men of ability, proportionate to their ability."

Page and his political partner, Leonidas Lafayette Polk, advocated for the establishment of a college for common citizens, and open public schools for all children, both blacks and whites.

As mentioned above, this inclusion of black children in North Carolina's public education system, by the Republicans in 1894, opened the political pathway for the counterattack by the Bourbon Democrats, in 1898.

As noted by Paul Escott, in Many Excellent People, in 1890, North Carolina had more illiterate whites than any other state, and 36% of the total population could not read.

The Bourbon Democrats found this level of structural ignorance politically valuable in maintaining control, and despised the idea that common citizens would obtain a publicly funded education.

Escott noted that when the,

 "violent response to democratic change came, (in 1898), not only did it confirm that racism was widespread, it also revealed that class purposes underlay racism and used it to restore the hierarchy that denied all forms of equality in society."

In an irony of history, after the Democrats overthrew the elected government in the coup d'etat in North Carolina in 1898, the governor who had the most to do with creating the political racial apartheid is revered by state historians as "North Carolina's education governor."

One of the goals for the Republican Populists of free common education was the creation of a "commonwealth of independent producers."

They took their goals on education from Jefferson, who advocated universal education as the bedrock for a democratic republic.

Shared Cultural Values and Faith in God.

In his sermons warning against the implementation of the Democrat White Man's Rule, John Kilgo, the President of Trinity College, from 1894 - 1910, preached that,

"God sets no limits upon the rights of men to know the truth, but rather stirs them with the energies of His spirit to search it out. God, of all beings, has little patience with, or tolerance of, a timid search for the truth."

The God that the Populists thought existed was the source of human nature and endowed human nature with a truth-seeking morality.

As described by Richard Tuck, in Natural Rights Theories, the Populists thought that man's relationship to each other was conceptually the same as God's relationship with each individual human.

Individuals, by using all of their intellectual and spiritual resources, could create God's Kingdom on earth. The relationship between God and man, in the Populist theology, was a reciprocal one between equals, which generated rights and obligations on both sides.

The Populist thought that this reciprocity and obligation in equal rights extended, naturally, to constitutional and political relationships.

As noted in Bruce Palmer's book, Man Over Money, the Populists would often invoke the teaching of Jesus in their political advocacy of reform.

"Christ did not come," said one Populist leader in 1894,

"as our theological quacks are so fond of saying, to prepare men for another world, but to teach them how to rightly live in this one."

Dr. Cyrus Thompson said that Christianity was the,

"very genius of human freedom," and criticized the southern church for failing to support the Populists.

Marion Butler, the Populist leader from North Carolina, said,

"A Christianity that cannot go down to the root causes from which poverty and oppression come is a stench in the nostrils of Jesus Christ."

As Micheal Zuckert described it in The Natural Rights Republic, the Populist interpretation of God means accepting the universal truths contained in the Declaration of Independence.

Those truths were held, by Jefferson, to be self-evident, meaning outside of a chain of logic, and not derived from any other propositions.

They are held to be,

"...self-evident within the political community dedicated to making them effective."

The most elemental value held by the Populists was that the core of the moral teachings in the Judeo-Christian heritage was that individual morality was built into human reason.

Jeffrey Reiman in Justice and Modern Moral Philosophy, describes how the synthesis of Jewish and Christian thought begins with the notion that,

 "the moral law is in fact built into the reason of every human being."

In other words, the Populists had faith in God, and so must any new constitutional arrangement that seeks to implement political reform based upon the ideology of individualism.

Conclusion: Towards a Constitutional Democratic Republic.

The political deck of cards dealt to citizens by Madison and Hamilton is stacked against reform of the existing constitution in Article V.

Nothing good is going to happen in reclaiming the American Democratic Impulse until and unless the citizens revoke Madison's special interest system.

Reforming Madison's system, through the amendments suggested by Levin, are inadequate for regaining the American democratic impulse of freedom.

And, progress on obtaining the common constitutional purpose of individual freedom will not be obtained until citizens gain greater control over the process of government and the ability to protect their rights.

And that progress means starting over again by creating a new constitutional democratic republic, beginning at the point in history of Jefferson's Declaration.

Bibliography.

Adams, John, The Political Writings of John Adams: Representative Selections, Edited with an Introduction by George A. Peek, Jr., New York, Liberal Arts Press, 1954.

Arrow, Kenneth Joseph, Social Choice and Individual Values, New York, Wiley, 1951.

Ayers, Edward L., The Promise of the New South: Life After Reconstruction, New York, Oxford University Press, 1992.

Bass, Jack, and DeVries, Walter, The Transformation of Southern Politics: Social Change and Political Consequence Since 1945, Athens, University of Georgia Press, 1995.

Bassett, John Spencer, Slavery in the State of North Carolina, Baltimore, Johns Hopkins Press, 1899, New York, AMS Press, 1972.

Beard, Charles Austin, The Economic Origins of Jeffersonian Democracy, New York, Macmillan Co., 1915.

Bernstein, Richard B., The Founding Fathers: A Very Short Introduction, Oxford University Press, 2015.

Billings, Dwight B., Planters and the Making of a "New South": Class, Politics, and Development in North Carolina, 1865-1900, Chapel Hill, University of North Carolina Press, 1979.

Blau, Peter Michael, Exchange and Power in Social Life, New York, J. Wiley, 1964.

Brennan, Geoffrey, and Buchanan, James M., The Reason of Rules: Constitutional Political Economy, Cambridge, New York, Cambridge University Press, 1985.

Buchanan, James M., Constitutional Economics, Oxford, UK., Cambridge, Mass., Blackwell, 1991.

Buchanan, James M., Theory of Public Choice: Political Applications of Economics, Ann Arbor, University of Michigan Press, 1972.

Buchanan, James, M., and Tullock, Gordon, The Calculus of Consent: Logical Foundations for Constitutional Democracy, The University of Michigan Press, 1962.

Busby, Josh, Evolution of North Carolina's Economic Development, Honors Essay: Dept. of Political Science, University of North Carolina at Chapel Hill, 1993.

Cash, W. J. (Wilbur Joseph), The Mind of the South: 1900-1941, 1st ed., New York, Alfred A. Knopf, 1941.

Cecil-Fronsman, Bill, Common Whites: Class and Culture In Antebellum, Lexington, KY., University Press of Kentucky, 1992.

Clayton, Bruce D., The Savage Ideal: Intolerance and Intellectual Leadership in the South, 1890-1914, Baltimore, Johns Hopkins University Press, 1972.

Crossan, John Dominic, The Historical Jesus: The Life of a Mediterranean Jewish Peasant, 1st ed., San Francisco, Harper, 1991.

Dahl, Robert A., How Democratic Is The American Constitution? 2cd ed., New Haven, Yale University Press, 2003.

Degler, Carl N., The Other South: Southern Dissenters in the Nineteenth Century, 1st ed., New York, Harper & Row, 1974.

Douglass, Elisha P., Rebels and Democrats: The Struggle for Equal Political Rights and Majority Rule During the American Revolution, Chapel Hill, University of North Carolina Press, 1955.

Escott, Paul D., Many Excellent People: Power and Privilege in North Carolina, 1850¬1900, Chapel Hill, University of North Carolina Press, 1985.

Genovese, Eugene D., The Slaveholders' Dilemma: Freedom and Progress in Southern Conservative Thought, 1820-1860, Columbia, S.C., University of South Carolina Press, 1992.

Goldwin, Robert A., From Parchment to Power: How James Madison Used the Bill of Rights to Save the Constitution, Washington, DC, AEI Press, 1997.

Goodwyn, Lawrence. Democratic Promise: The Populist Moment in America, New York, Oxford University Press, 1976.

Granovetter, Mark and Swedberg, Richard, The Sociology of Economic Life, Boulder, Westview Press, 1992.

Hahn, Steven, The Roots of Southern Populism: Yeomen Farmers and the Transformation of the Georgia Upcountry,

1850-1890, New York, Oxford University Press, 1983.

Hamilton, Alexander, Madison, James, and Jay, John, The Federalist: A Collection of Essays Written in Favor of the New Constitution as Agreed Upon by the Federal Convention, September September 17, 1787, Reprinted from the original text under the editorial supervision of Henry B. Dawson. Essays written by Alexander Hamilton, James Madison and John Jay under pseudonym of "Publius".

Harnack, Adolf von, What is Christianity? Lectures Delivered in the University of Berlin During the Winter-term, 1899-1900, 2cd ed., rev. New York, G. P. Putnam's Sons, London, Williams and Norgate, 1901.

Hart, Albert Bushnell, The Southern South, New York, London, D. Appleton and Company, 1910.

Hill, Stuart, Democratic Values and Technological Choices, Stanford, Calif., Stanford University Press, 1992.

Hobbes, Thomas, Leviathan, London, J.M. Dent & Sons, Ltd., New York, E.P. Dutton & Co. [n.d.].

Hunt, E. K., History of Economic Thought: A Critical Perspective, Belmont, Calif., Wadsworth Pub. Co., 1979.

Jensen, Merrill, The Articles of Confederation: An Interpretation of the Social-Constitutional History of the American Revolution, 1774-1781. University of Wisconsin Press, 1959.

Jensen, Merrill, The Making of the American Constitution, D. Van Nostrand Co., Inc., Princeton, N.J., 1964.

Key, V. O. (Vladimer Orlando),with the assistance of Alexander Heard, Southern Politics in State and Nation, New York, A. A. Knopf, 1949.

Keynes, John Maynard,. The General Theory of Employment, Interest and Money, New York, Harcourt, Brace, 1935.

Lefler, Hugh Talmage, Newsome, Albert R., North Carolina: The History of A Southern State, Chapel Hill, UNC Press, 1973.

Levin, Mark, The Liberty Amendments, Restoring the American Republic, Threshold, 2014.

Locke, John, The Second Treatise of Government (An Essay Concerning the True Original, Extent and End of Civil Government), and A Letter Concerning Toleration, edited by Charles L. Sherman, New York, Irvington, 1979.

Macpherson, C. B. (Crawford Brough), The Political Theory of Possessive Individualism: Hobbes to Locke, Oxford, Clarendon Press, 1962.

McAdams, Robert McCormick, Paths of Fire: An Anthropologist's Inquiry into Western Technology, Princeton, N.J., Princeton University Press, 1996.

McDonald, Forrest, Novus Ordo Seclorum: The Intellectual Origins of the Constitution, Lawrence, Kan., University Press of Kansas, 1985.

McMath, Robert C., Populist Vanguard: A History of the Southern Farmers' Alliance, New York, Norton, 1975.

Meyers, Marvin, The Mind of the Founder: Sources of the Political Thought of James Madison, Hanover, N.H., Published for Brandeis University Press by University Press of New England, 1981.

Miles, Jack, God: A Biography, 1st ed.,
New York, Alfred A. Knopf, 1995.

Mill, John Stuart, Utilitarianism, Liberty,
and Representative Government, Hackett
Publishing Company, Inc., 1996.

Nathans, Sydney, The Quest for Progress:
The Way We Lived in North Carolina:
1870¬1920, Chapel Hill, University of
North Carolina Press, 1983.

Newby, I. A. (Idus A.), Plain Folk in the
New South: Social Change and Cultural
Persistence, 1880-1915, Baton Rouge,
Louisiana State University Press, 1989.

Noblin, Stuart, Leonidas LaFayette Polk: A
Study in Agrarian Leadership Chapel Hill,
University of North Carolina Press, 1949.

Olsen, Otto, Reconstruction and
Redemption in the South, Baton Rouge,
Louisiana State University Press, 1980.

Palmer, Bruce, Man Over Money: The
Southern Populist Critique of American
Capitalism, Chapel Hill, University of
North Carolina Press, 1980.

Perman, Michael, The Road to
Redemption: Southern Politics, 1869-1879,
Chapel Hill, University of North Carolina
Press, 1984.

Peterson, Merrill D., The Jefferson Image in the American Mind, New York, Oxford University Press, 1960.

Rakove, Jack N., Declaring Rights : A Brief History with Documents, Boston, Bedford Books, 1998.

Rawls, John, A Theory of Justice, Cambridge, Mass., Belknap Press of Harvard University Press, 1971.

Reiman, Jeffrey H., Justice and Modern Moral Philosophy, New Haven, Yale University Press, 1990.

Schwartz, Michael, Radical Protest and Social Structure: The Southern Farmers' Alliance and Cotton Tenancy, 1880-1890, New York, Academic Press, 1976.

Schweikart, Larry, Banking in the American South from the Age of Jackson to Reconstruction, Baton Rouge, Louisiana State University Press, 1987.

Sheehan, Thomas, The First Coming: How the Kingdom of God Became Christianity, 1st ed., New York, Random House, 1986.

Smith, Adam, An Inquiry into the Nature and Causes of the Wealth of Nations, Oxford, Clarendon Press, 1976.

Schweikart, Larry, Banking in the American South from the Age of Jackson to Reconstruction, LSU Press, 1987.).

Tillich, Paul, A History of Christian Thought: From Is Judaic and Hellenistic Origins to Existentialism, New York, Simon and Schuster, 1972.

Tocqueville, Alexis de, Democracy in America. The Henry Reeve Text as revised by Francis Bowen, now further corr. and edited with a historical essay, editorial notes, and bibliographies by Phillips Bradley, New York, Vintage Books, 1954.

Tuck, Richard, Natural Rights Theories: Their Origins and Development, Cambridge, Cambridge University Press, 1979.

Tullos, Allen, Habits of Industry: White Culture and the Transformation of the Carolina Piedmont, Chapel Hill, University of North Carolina Press, 1989.

Wilentz, Sean, The Rise of American Democracy: Jefferson to Lincoln, New York, W. W. Norton & Co., Inc., 2005.

Wood, Gordon S., The Creation of the American Republic: 1776-1787, Chapel Hill, Published for the Institute of Early American History and Culture at Williamsburg, Va., by the University of North Carolina Press, 1969.

Wood, Phillip J., Southern Capitalism: The Political Economy of North Carolina, 1880¬1980, Durham, N.C., Duke University Press, 1986.

Woodward, C. Vann, (Comer Vann), Origins of The New South, 1877-1913, 1st ed., Baton Rouge, LA., Louisiana State University Press, 1951.

Wright, Gavin, Old South, New South: Revolutions in the Southern Economy Since the Civil War, New York, Basic Books, 1986.

Zuckert, Michael P., The Natural Rights Republic: Studies in the Foundation of the American Political Tradition, Rev. ed., Notre Dame, Indiana., University of Notre Dame Press, 1996.